Praise for *The Anxious Christian*

I loved this book. I often read something and think, this will be helpful to many, but I can't think of anyone who would not be helped by reading Rhett's book. It made me smile to see once more how God tucks the best news inside the most unusual boxes if we have the courage to open them.

> —**SHEILA WALSH**, author of *God Loves Broken People and Those Who Pretend They're Not*

Rhett Smith asks Christians to stop and take seriously how God is using anxiety in their life. Rhett's an extraordinarily able pastor and counselor, and his surprising new take on the anxious Christian should be in the hands of every "3 AMer" out there.

> —**HUGH HEWITT**, nationally syndicated talk show host and author

For the first time, I see my anxiety as something to press into rather than run from. The Anxious Christian *bears the same gifts as many of my favorite books: an earnest voice, a fresh perspective, and an invitation to begin a journey.*

> —**SCOTT MCCLELLAN**, writer, editor, and director of the ECHO Conference

In these pages, the reader will read a truthful and vulnerable account of how the author has the courage and presence to use anxiety to point himself and his relationships toward the effort to change his own identity and patterns. Read slowly and re-read—you will be rewarded with wisdom that has a practical application of change in your journey of life.

> —**DR. TERRY HARGRAVE**, author and professor of marriage and family therapy at Fuller Seminary

THE ANXIOUS CHRISTIAN

CAN GOD USE YOUR ANXIETY FOR GOOD?

RHETT SMITH

MOODY PUBLISHERS

CHICAGO

All Scripture quotations, unless otherwise indicated, are taken from the *Holy Bible, New International Version*®, NIV®. Copyright ©1973, 1978, 1984 by Biblica, Inc.™ Used by permission of Zondervan. All rights reserved worldwide.

Scripture quotations marked NASB are taken from the *New American Standard Bible*®, Copyright ©1960, 1962, 1963, 1968, 1971, 1972, 1973, 1975, 1977, 1995 by The Lockman Foundation. Used by permission. (www.Lockman.org)

Scripture quotations marked NRSV are from the *New Revised Standard Version* of the Bible, copyright 1989, by the Division of Christian Education of the National Council of the Churches of Christ in the USA. Used by permission. All rights reserved.

All websites listed herein are accurate at the time of publication, but may change in the future or cease to exist. The listing of website references and resources does not imply publisher endorsement of the site's entire contents. Groups, corporations, and organizations are listed for informational purposes, and listing does not imply publisher endorsement of their activities.

Details related to counseling clients have been changed to protect their privacy.

Editor: Christopher Reese   Cover Design: Erik M. Peterson
Interior Design: Ragont Design

Library of Congress Cataloging-in-Publication Data

Smith, Rhett.
    The anxious Christian : can God use your anxiety for good? / Rhett Smith.
        p. cm.
    Includes bibliographical references (p.   ).
    ISBN 978-0-8024-1322-2
    1. Anxiety—Religious aspects—Christianity. 2. Christian life. I. Title.
BV4908.5.S653 2011
248.8'6—dc23

                                                                    2011044694

We hope you enjoy this book from Moody Publishers. Our goal is to provide high-quality, thought-provoking books and products that connect truth to your real needs and challenges. For more information on other books and products written and produced from a biblical perspective, go to www.moodypublishers.com or write to:

Moody Publishers
820 N. LaSalle Boulevard
Chicago, IL 60610

3 5 7 9 10 8 6 4 2

Printed in the United States of America

To my mother, Melodee, who courageously
faced her anxiety in the midst of her breast cancer.

To my father, Tim, brother, Wyatt, and Rita, who have
been the best traveling companions on this journey.

To my beautiful children, Hayden and Hudson, who have
taught me more about facing my fears than anyone.

Last, to my extraordinary wife, Heather—no words can
ever convey just how much you have transformed my life.
I would not be who I am today, if not for you. I love you.

"Those who believe that they believe in God,
but without passion in their hearts, without anguish
in their mind, without uncertainty, without doubt,
without an element of despair even in their consolation,
believe only in the God idea, not God Himself."
Spanish philosopher and writer, MIGUEL DE UNAMUNO[1]

Join the Conversation
(theanxiouschristian.com)
rhettsmith.com
Twitter: @rhetter #anxiouschristian
Facebook: http://www.facebook.com/pages/
Rhett-Smith/253756434643419

contents

foreword

Someday, I hope someone writes a book called *The Amazingly Confident Christian* and asks me to write the foreword. Or the *Surprisingly Adept at Pop-N-Lock Christian*. I'm ready to lend my name to either one of those projects, but for now writing the foreword for *The Anxious Christian* makes perfect sense.

Truthfully, my breakdancing skills have lost their *Breakin' 2: Electric Boogalo* luster, and I've wrestled with anxiety in my life.

One of the ways I see that manifest itself is when I see or hear a door close at work. My first assumption, the very first thought that blossoms in my head is, "Somebody is having a closed-door meeting to talk about firing me."

It doesn't matter if I don't know those particular team members. It doesn't matter if work is going splendidly and my performance that year has been amazing. It doesn't matter if there's a whiteboard full of ideas that are clearly not about me. My gut reaction to a door closing is, "Better go ahead and pack up my stuff because I'll be gone by the end of the day."

That can't be normal.

That can't be healthy.

That can't be good.

But that's what I think. And, usually, I think I'm the only one who feels that way. That's one of anxiety's greatest tricks —it tries to isolate you, to put you on an island by yourself, to make you believe that everyone else has it all figured out except you. You're the weird one. Better bottle that fear up and hide it. Better not tell anyone you're feeling anxious. Better start to use the Christian F word: "Fine."

How's your marriage? Fine!

How's your job? Fine!

How's your family? Fine!

And if you say "fine" enough, you start to become two people: anxious and worrisome on the inside, shiny and fake on the outside.

That's why books like *The Anxious Christian* are so important to me and millions of other people. This book cuts through the fakeness and fear. Part memoir and part manual, it offers real hope for real people who often have real worries.

I didn't just write this foreword for Rhett because he's my friend. I didn't write it because they paid me a tremendous amount of money—and spinning rims don't just pay for themselves.

I wrote this foreword because this was a book I needed, and I think other people need it too.

—Jon Acuff, author of *Quitter: Closing the Gap Between Your Day Job & Your Dream Job*

The Day I Became a Stutterer

"Life is difficult."[1]

M. SCOTT PECK, *The Road Less Traveled*

I have been living with anxiety for about as long as I can remember.

On September 9, 1981, the morning after my grandfather's funeral, my mother felt a lump in her breast. It was breast cancer. I was six years old.

"Your wife has a wild, fast growing cancer that may have already spread to her liver and brain," a surgeon told my father. And so the anxiety began.

"If she lives more than six weeks, it will be a miracle," my mother's oncologist said to my father, as she told him how her lungs were now riddled with cancer and pneumonia.

"If you don't tell Melodee, I will."

So in September of 1985 my mom sat my brother Wyatt and me down in her hospital room. She asked us if we knew why Jesus had come to earth. I don't remember what I said, but my dad would later tell me that I answered that He came "to be our Savior, so that we could go to heaven."

My mom said, "Yes, that's right, and it's about time for me to go to heaven."

This news forever altered the course of my life as anxiety began its insidious work on a daily basis. In the beginning my anxiety took the form of worry, as I constantly wondered if, and when, my mom would die. But as a child full of faith and trust in God, I often found my worry overshadowed by my overwhelming belief that God would never let my mom die. God doesn't take away the people we love, I repeatedly told myself.

And then at the age of eleven, several months after my mom told me that she was dying, I was playing soccer in the backyard with my younger brother, Wyatt. I can picture that scene so vividly. Through the back patio sliding door I could see my mom, dad, and one of my mom's best friends preparing lunch in the kitchen. It is a crystal clear memory that has taken up permanent residence in the forefront of my mind. A memory that I replay from time to time.

I remember my father and my mom's friend coming outside and calling us to come sit down with them.

"The doctors have given your mom one month to live."

My mom slipped in and out of a coma in that final week before her five-year battle with breast cancer took her life at the age of thirty-nine.

That was the day that anxiety became a permanent travel companion on my life journey.

After my mom died, life would never be the same. I lived in a perpetual state of worry and panic. I began to develop rituals as a way to quell the growing anxiety that I felt as an adolescent. And I avoided any situation that made me feel out of control. In an attempt to assert some type of control in my life, I developed compulsive habits like touching door handles a certain number of times, or making sure I had counted all the tiles on a ceiling before I left a room. As long as I counted any number of items that crossed my path, I believed no one else I loved would die. But if I failed to count the items, then I believed I would lose another loved one to death. It was a twisted and distorted game that I played with God as a child. A game that always left me tied up in knots of anxiety.

What many people who know me now may not realize is that I am a stutterer. Two weeks after my mom died, I went back to school. It was like any Monday, except that my family life had been forever changed, and to my surprise, I found that I could no longer read out loud in class. I went from an outgoing fifth-grade student who loved to read to a shy, cautious little kid who was afraid to be called on to read aloud.

All I wanted to do was hide inside myself, for fear of others finding out that I was somehow weak, or a failure. The apostle Paul's words to the Corinthians that God's strength is present in our weakness didn't resonate with me as an eleven-year-old who had just lost his mom to breast cancer. I did not feel God's strength. I only felt my weakness.

I felt so much shame and embarrassment that I could not even read a simple sentence out loud. When called upon to read, I knew that at best I would be humiliated. My classmates would only hear pathetic puffs of air escaping out of my mouth as I desperately tried to pronounce a word from one of the sentences staring back at me from the page.

That feeling of inadequacy caused me to withdraw inside myself, and I would often pretend during class that I did not know where we were during our group reading time. As each student took their turn I felt my chest tighten and found it harder and harder to breathe as my turn to read inched closer. When the time came, I chose to have my name put on the board as punishment rather than trying to muster up the courage to read out loud in front of my classmates. This inward shame was manifesting itself now in public humiliation.

Most of my life has been lived in fear of reading out loud and being a slave to performing the correct rituals to hold off the anxiety long enough so that I could try to feel normal. I just wanted to fit in and not be noticed for what I believed was a major flaw in who I was. I wondered why God would allow one of His creations to struggle so much with anxiety and live in the shame that resulted from it.

But something slowly began to change in my life as I realized I could no longer be a prisoner to anxiety. That was no way to live. I was a junior in college trying to carefully navigate the transition between adolescence and young adulthood. I knew that I had to begin making some different choices for my life. Otherwise I would forever be captive to the tyranny of my fears.

In hindsight I cannot honestly tell you whether this decision to change course was a conscious or unconscious choice. But what I do know is that God was at work in my life, and it was He who was coming alongside of me. He was helping me to begin seeing anxiety as a tool for growth in my life, rather than the source of pain it had always been. Viewing anxiety as a negative force only left me paralyzed in a prison of fear and shame. I was tired of living in fear of failure, worrying about other people's opinions about whether I was good enough. But viewing anxiety as a catalyst for growth in my life could set me free to take more risks, and help me to become more of who I believe God created me to be.

The remarkable Christian philosopher Søren Kierkegaard talks at length in his writings about a *leap of faith*[2] that is set in motion by anxiety. He describes it as an anxiety that is rooted in our freedom—"Anxiety is always to be understood as oriented toward freedom."[3] I would later come to see that God had planned to use my anxiety as a catalyst to set me free.

I can still remember the day as if it were happening right now. I was in my campus apartment pacing around the living room full of worry and fear. My relationship with my longtime girlfriend seemed to be heading in the wrong direction. My major in psychology no longer seemed to interest me. And I was worried that I wouldn't be able to get a job after college. I was in the midst of all of these major transitions and my life seemed to be falling apart.

Anxiety is not content in just residing in one area of a person's life, but instead forcefully invades as much of a person's being as possible. My fears about reading out loud had over time permeated other areas of my life, creating a sense of anxiousness that was always below the surface. What had begun as a fear of reading in front of others soon spread to a fear of having conversations with others—alarmed that I might trip up over a word that I should have been able to easily pronounce. In class, teachers would sometimes step in and try to help me, but most of the time they seemed as helpless as I felt. Being a stutterer in school felt lonely. Each interaction I had was full of anxiety as the possibility of stuttering was always present, which continued to reinforce the negative beliefs that I was starting to construct about myself.

If you have never struggled with an anxiety such as this, it may be hard for you to imagine. But my anxiousness regarding any verbal interaction began to seriously inhibit my social interaction—perhaps that's why most of my friends thought I was just shy. But they didn't realize that part of my shyness was my attempt to not put myself in situations where I would be humiliated. If I could avoid talking on the phone, then I would. I still remember calling up a girl that I had a crush on in the sixth grade. As I placed that call my heart raced with fear as I hoped I could be able to clearly enunciate to whoever answered the phone my desire to speak with her. After much stuttering I was eventually able to spit out her name to the person who answered the phone, but I still heard his muffled voice as he made fun of me to the people who were with him in the house. Interactions like that left me doubting my ability to successfully navigate life, especially during what was already a difficult adolescence.

Not all of my conversations were filled with anxiety or stuttering, which may be why so many people never knew I was so painfully struggling inside. Even in the midst of my difficulties there were moments of grace where I felt God intervene and help me get through a difficult conversation. And usually, once I was able to break through the first few words, it was almost like I was able to begin a good flow and speak with confidence. I would talk for hours on the phone with my friends in high school, never feeling that anxiety except for some sparse moments. But the start-up was what was so painful.

But I had a growing sense that if I was ever going to be able to not feel like a failure in life, and if God was ever going to be able to use me, then I was going to need to deal with my fear of reading and speaking out loud. If my spreading anxiety could possibly ever be contained, then it would have to begin with what I was most afraid of. The details are fuzzy to me, but I remember reading through some writings of A.W. Tozer one day during my junior year in college. I don't remember what I read, but I remember feeling that I needed to take a risk.

As I stood in the living room I muttered under my breath to God, "Just give me a chance to speak! Just give me any opportunity and use me. If You do, I will take it. I will face my anxiety, but You have to help me!"

It was one of those prayers that I believe we are yearning to say, but we are so fearful of the implications of those words as they depart from our lips. But it may have been one of the most honest and vulnerable prayers I have ever uttered to God. I am finding that those prayers of complete abandonment to Him are very rare in my spiritual life.

For ten years I had been living in fear of speaking in front of others. My prayer was a desperate cry. It was a feeling of absolute and terrifying freedom to give this over to God, and I wondered what awaited me at the end of that prayer. Would

He reach out and respond? Would He catch me on the other end of my anxious leap?

About two weeks later I picked up the ringing phone in my apartment.

"Hello. Ummm, no, but thanks for the offer. And thanks for thinking of me." That was my automatic and instinctual response. Dave Septer who was the Student Life Director at Grand Canyon University in Phoenix, Arizona, wanted to know if I would be willing to speak at the Easter morning sunrise service on our college campus. Even as I was hanging up the phone, the voices in my head began to spew out all the negative beliefs I had about myself, and the anxiety intensified. All the feelings of inadequacy and humiliation rose to the surface in an instant and triggered my usual coping mechanisms. My gut instinct was to withdraw and move away from anything that involved risk.

In my head, I heard, *"Are you kidding me, why would they ask you to speak to a bunch of people, especially on such an important day? You can't speak, you can barely talk, and you can hardly read out loud. You are inadequate. You are not good enough. You will embarrass yourself. Say no and stay home!"*

But all of a sudden the negative messages stopped, the voices died down, and I heard another voice. This voice was different, and the clarity by which it spoke to the inner recesses of my heart, soul, and mind felt almost palpable.

And then I felt I heard God say these words specifically to me.

"Isn't this the exact opportunity you prayed for only two weeks ago?"

And that was it.

I don't remember anything else except believing that God was now offering up the possibility for me to look my own anxiety in the face and push through the resistance that it had continually been exerting on me up to this point in my life. And so I agreed to speak.

The next several weeks were filled with worry, a nervous stomach, and lots of anxious, restless nights. I prepared harder for that sermon than almost any other that I have ever prepared for. All I could do was be faithful to the opportunity God had given me. After that, He would have to work through my anxiety if I was going to be able to say anything at all on that early Easter morning.

Easter morning of 1996 came quickly. My roommate, Eric, laughed when I set three alarms that night so that I wouldn't oversleep. But if you've ever had to wake up early for an important event, then you know I hardly slept at all that night. I rose early to practice my lines, but everything always sounds great when one is practicing alone. How would it actually turn out when I began speaking to a couple hundred of my peers?

On the day of Jesus' resurrection, God used my anxiety to breathe new life into me. A little less than 2,000 years ago Jesus did the unimaginable by rising from the dead, and in doing so came alongside the anxious hearts of His worried disciples and followers. In that very act He helped set them on a new course in life to face the challenges and take the risks that would arise before them. Challenges that they might have been tempted to hide from if God hadn't shaped their anxiety in a life-transforming way. That same God would take the anxiety that had held me captive for the last ten years and flip it upside down and use it as a catalyst for change in my life.

I would like to tell you that I delivered a compelling sermon like Tim Keller. But I didn't. I would like to tell you that up there on stage, in front of my peers, I was as engaging as Jon Acuff. But I wasn't. I painfully struggled to produce the sounds of the first word of my sermon.

I stuttered.

And I stopped.

And I started again.

And I stuttered.

And I stopped again.

This was the vicious cycle that I had been used to for so many years.

There is a very powerful scene in the movie *The King's Speech*[4] where King George VI, played by Colin Firth, delivers a speech in 1939 at Buckingham Palace, declaring war with Germany. King George VI struggles through each and every word of the speech. It's a powerful scene, but as a stutterer it created a very intense, visceral reaction deep inside my chest. That fear of failing in front of everyone and embarrassing yourself in front of your peers and strangers is how I felt that day. It is a very real and terrifying moment when anxiety does everything it can to devour you alive.

As I stood there speechless I began wondering if I might have misheard God's voice.

But if you recall from that scene in *The King's Speech*,

King George VI's speech therapist, Lionel Logue, is there to slowly and patiently coach the king through each and every word. On that day God was there coaching me through every anxious moment. It's not that the anxiety stopped, or that the fear subsided as I preached that sermon. Rather, in the midst of my panic I felt like God gave me a glimpse that life could look different. There was now hope that I could face my fears and begin to work through them. There was hope that I didn't have to feel alone in my anxiety. I rushed through that sermon at a fast rate, hoping that if I didn't slow down and pause too long, the momentum of my speaking would help carry me along stutter-free. Like much of my battle with anxiety, that sermon was a very confusing time. There was such a mixture of joy in the opportunity to talk before others and share my life and the work that God was doing—but coupled with the fear that the very next word could send my voice into paralysis.

Like many of the talks I have given since I have always been my harshest critic. But something was birthed in me that day as others came forward thanking me for sharing my story with them. And no one mentioned my stuttering, even when I brought it up. Perhaps God was at work.

And so on April 7, 1996, as I began to talk about resurrection and new life, I also began to reflect back on the memory of my mom who had died on April 20, 1986.

God, who had raised His Son Jesus from the dead and brought Him new life, had also raised my mom from the dead and given her new life in eternity. And He would now bring me new life. God was helping me rewrite a new story through my anxiety. For so long I had feared pursuing what He had been calling me to do, and who He had been calling me to be. On that day He would transform my anxiety into a life-giving force that would help me pursue Him even in the midst of my most anxiety-filled times.

When I took that step, and stood up to speak that day, God did not remove my anxiety. But He set in motion my journey of starting to see anxiety as a tool for growth in my life, and as a catalyst to spur me beyond the limitations and the fears that I hid behind.

You might find yourself full of all kinds of anxiety, worry, and panic. And those feelings might be keeping you captive and holding you back from the abundant life God is calling you into.

Maybe you've experienced death and disease, divorce and conflict, physical and emotional trauma. And maybe those things have stirred up so much anxiety in you that you don't know if you can step out and take any more risks.

Or maybe you find yourself in the midst of some major life transitions, and all the options before you have you paralyzed in the grip of anxiety.

But I want you to know that God is not finished with us. He has only just begun. And if we take the risk and step out in faith, He is there to guide our anxiety toward a fruitful endeavor in order that we may grow into the person He desires us to become.

Wherever you are in life, and whatever you have experienced, I'm here to encourage you today, and to tell you that you can do this. You can face your anxiety, and God can use it in a way that breathes new life into you.

Will you please join me on this journey? What are you waiting for?

chapter one

Embracing Anxiety

"If there's anyone who can appear before Aslan without their knees knocking, they're either braver than most or just silly."[1]

C. S. LEWIS, *The Lion, the Witch, and the Wardrobe*

I f you were to come to my home and walk into my study you would find two sets of *The Chronicles of Narnia* proudly sitting on the top of my bookshelves. One set I bought for Christmas of 2006, a gift for my wife in hopes that we would one day read this wonderful book series to the child we were expecting the following summer. And next to the newer version is an older, well-worn set that belonged to my mother. It's a set that I cherish because she used to read it to me as a child. In fact, *The Lion, the Witch, and the Wardrobe* is one of my last memories of her reading a book with me. It was in those early readings that my mom, through the words of C. S. Lewis, introduced me to the terrifying but loving lion, Aslan.

Meeting Aslan as a child left an indelible mark on my imagination and it was one of the earliest images that I most identified God with. There was this sense growing up that God, like the lion Aslan, could be quite scary. But it was not a scariness that drove me to run away from Him. Rather, the scared feelings I felt seemed only to have propelled me toward Him.

Looking back now, I can see that as a child I had this sense of anxiety about God. It's still very much present in my relationship with Him today. So I can identify with Susan in *The Lion, the Witch, and the Wardrobe* who in her anxiety is questioning Mr. Beaver on whether or not Aslan is safe. What she finds out is that he isn't safe, but instead that he is good. "'Then he isn't safe?' said Lucy. 'Safe?' said Mr. Beaver; 'don't you hear what Mrs. Beaver tells you? Who said anything about safe? Course he isn't safe. But he's good. He's the king I tell you.'"[2]

And so I began to see my anxiety as something that didn't always feel safe. It brought up feelings and emotions that I didn't like to deal with and it made me question all kinds of things going on in my life. I would do anything to stuff those feelings deep down inside of me in hopes that they would never reappear. But in its lack of safety I slowly began to see that my anxiety was good and led me to pursue God more than I ever had. I was beginning to see that God didn't want me to stuff those emotions and feelings and so He used anxiety as a tool in my life to help me more radically pursue Him and who He wanted me to become.

I know that your anxiety is scary and that it does not feel safe.

But what if your anxiety can be used for good?

What if God has allowed anxiety in your life in hopes that you wouldn't continue to stuff and bury every feeling and emotion that you experience?

How would perceiving anxiety in this way begin to change how you live?

Fear of Anxiety

It is more than likely that if you have ever taken the risk to share your anxiety within the Christian community, you have heard some counsel in the form of the apostle Paul's exhortation in Philippians 4:6. Paul says to the "holy people" at Phillipi, "Do not be anxious about anything." It's a very powerful verse, a favorite of mine, and one that Christians have turned to time and time again when they experience anxiousness. Perhaps you have used it when trying to encourage others during their times of anxiety.

I believe that when we cite this as the cure-all to one's anxiety we mean very well. In fact, many find comfort with the recitation of these six simple words. But in our attempts to help others and perhaps deflect our own anxiety and feelings of helplessness, we can inadvertently communicate the wrong message.

Often a Christian will come to counseling and tell me that they have tried to follow the "biblical counsel" of others to not be anxious, but their anxiety doesn't quite seem to dissipate.

"Is something wrong with me? Am I a bad Christian?" they desperately ask me.

"No, nothing is wrong with you," I tell them. "What if God is using your anxiety to speak to you? What might God be saying to you?" I ask.

When we discourage others from safely expressing their anxiety, then we are essentially saying to them that anxiety is a bad emotion, and that it is something to be done away with. It communicates to them that perhaps something is wrong with their Christian faith and they begin to internalize the message, "I'm a Christian. I'm not supposed to be anxious."

Kierkegaard referred to anxiety as our "best teacher"[3] because of its ability to keep us in a struggle that strives for a solution, rather than opting to forfeit the struggle and slide into a possible depression. It would be nice if our lives and our Christian faith did not involve any struggle. But to believe that, and to perpetuate the belief to others that somehow the struggle with anxiety is unchristian, is a mistake.

We are not the first people to struggle with anxiety and the emotions that surround it. In fact, as Christians we come from a long line of people who have struggled with anxiety and have gone into hiding, putting on masks, and in the process have become less of who God created them to be. In the opening pages of Scripture we see that when Adam and Eve ate of the fruit from the tree of knowledge both of their eyes were opened. In that moment their instinct was to fight or flee, which is what most of us do when we are faced with anxiety. In their anxiousness, Adam and Eve chose to blame each other, flee from the scene, hide, and cover themselves up. I can only imagine the anxiety that the two of them must have felt as they hid from the Lord, waiting to be found out. Every sound coming from the Lord as He made his way toward them must have filled them with a growing sense of dread. As Scripture records,

Then the eyes of both of them were opened, and they realized they were naked; so they sewed fig leaves together and
made coverings for themselves. Then the man and his wife
heard the sound of the Lord God as he was walking in the
garden in the cool of the day, and they hid from the Lord
God among the trees of the garden. But the Lord God
called to the man, "Where are you?" He answered, "I heard
you in the garden, and I was afraid because I was naked; so I
hid." (Genesis 3:7–10)

When faced with anxiety we feel exposed, naked, and
vulnerable. Hiding and covering up is typically how we
respond when we feel those things.

God has not only created us, but He has created us as
free beings, and in our freedom we are given possibility and
choice. I would like for you for a moment to imagine God
freely calling you toward His good purposes. And as you
journey in that direction you may find yourself caught
between the present and the future. That in-between place of
present and future can create all kinds of anxiety because of
the freedom of choices God has given us in our life. Perhaps
we are anxious because the experiences of our past have
shaped us in such a way that we are in dread of making a free
and deliberate choice. Or perhaps just the mere possibility of
making a wrong choice has left you feeling anxious.

Anxiety is, therefore, both the cost and gift of our identity as free creatures in relationship to God. We have choices.
Without freedom, and the anxiety it entails, we are just
slaves—yearning for safety and security and grumbling at

God rather than living the anxious journey through the wilderness toward freedom.

Maybe during your life journey you feel as if the plans and purposes that God has for your life are not congruent with the life you are leading. And no matter how many times someone quotes to you Jeremiah 29:11 ("For I know the plans I have for you," declares the Lord, "plans to prosper you and not to harm you, plans to give you hope and a future"), you just don't feel at peace in your heart. What many people forget to tell you is that in verse 29:10 the Lord says that Israel will go through seventy years of exile and slavery in Babylon. Talk about anxiety! But God would use this time of trouble to draw Israel closer to Him. It was during this time of exile that God continually reminded His people that He was their God and that when they sought Him with all their heart He would listen and deliver them out of captivity.

Anxiety beckons us to not allow our lives to get stuck in a rut. If God gives us freedom and allows possibility, then just maybe God has hardwired anxiety into us as part of those choices. Perhaps anxiety is a paradoxical feeling offered up to us as a gift that propels us to seek after Him and to continually grow in the process.

Perhaps anxiety is an act of grace because it encourages us to face our fears, so that we can then choose to freely follow God where He is calling us to.

Embracing Anxiety

Discovering Anxiety Within

I remember a particular session one day with a young adult woman who was in her mid-twenties and really struggling with anxiety. She was worried and overwhelmed with life's choices and she felt stuck, unable to make a decision or move forward. I could see the look of desperation in her eyes as she sat frozen across from me on the couch. On the outside she looked calm and her college degree and successful career communicated that she was in control of her life. But under the surface her anxiety was screaming, "I don't know what to do! Help me!"

She, like many of us, struggles with a myriad of questions that we are constantly asking, and that leave us feeling anxious and unsure. In our anxiety we wrestle with questions like:

What if I fail?
Will my parents get divorced?
Can I find a career that I'm passionate about?
Should I marry this person?
What if I can't have kids?
Should we move or stay here?
Should I tell someone about my abuse?
How can a loving God allow me to have so much hurt in my life?

And others like them.

Some of the same questions persist, and new ones may arise over time. But under the surface we are wrestling with the basic questions that we face at each transitional stage in life: "Who am I?" "What am I to do?" "How am I to be loved?" and "How can I become all that God intended me to be?"[4] They are what the renowned psychiatrist Irvin D. Yalom refers to as our "ultimate concerns"[5]—freedom, isolation, belonging, and meaning. These questions are of the utmost importance and are often the driving force behind much of our anxiety. They strike at the heart of our identity and who we believe God created us to be. These questions are concerns shared by God as well. After all, He is the one who has stirred up these deep and pressing questions within us.

Anxiety manifests itself to each of us in its own unique way. It has the potential to be both helpful (butterflies before a talk, excitement before a first date, nervousness before you recite the wedding vows) and harmful (stress about making decisions, worry of being abandoned, fear of being intimate).[6] More commonly we may think of or experience anxiety in the forms of worry, fear, stress, guilt, shame, or dread. I like the way that anxiety researcher and psychologist Edmund Bourne describes four specific types of anxiety[7] in his *Anxiety and Phobia Workbook*. He talks about anxiety in the form of the Worrier,[8] Critic,[9] Victim,[10] and Perfectionist,[11] all categories that I believe resonate with different people's experiences of anxiety.

If you identify with those negative feelings of anxiety, then maybe it is time for you to open yourself up to see anxiety in a new and positive light. Anxiety can often indicate to us that there is something constructive happening within us, beckoning us to follow it in order that our lives may be transformed. I remember my churning stomach the very first time I lined up in the starting blocks to run the 300-meter hurdles in high school. I hoped that anxiety would eventually go away, but it didn't, and I came to realize that it was a feeling that helped me feel capable and ready to sprint from the blocks as fast as I could. Anxiety reminds us that we are alive, a feeling that is important in keeping us from going numb and withdrawing from the life God desires for us.

But how do you know if the anxiety you are experiencing is a healthy or unhealthy anxiety? That can be difficult to discern. Normal, healthy anxiety occurs when you confront the unknown, doubts arise, and the transitions ahead of you seem unclear. Healthy anxiety gives you the ability to say, "I can do it." But unhealthy anxiety is characterized by worry and an inability to make decisions in life, leading to mental and emotional paralysis. Healthy anxiety spurs us toward action, while unhealthy anxiety keeps us mired in inaction. We no longer feel we can do it, so we say and believe, "I can't, and I won't."

Anxiety is a part of our lives, but we don't have to let it keep us living in a prison of fear or retreating in shame. We have the opportunity to look it square in the face and allow God to use it to transform our lives.

Hiding in Shame

My daughter is intrigued with any person who puts on a mask, costume, or cape, and is intent on being one of the "good guys." She is obsessed with superheroes. When she was about three years old, she showed an affinity for Batman, so my wife and I decided to buy her a Batman mask and T-shirt. Every day she would faithfully put on that mask, grab her cape, and run around the house "fighting the bad guys." The more she immersed herself in the role, the more our families sent her all kinds of dress-up superhero costumes until we had quite an extensive array strewn about our house. She loved to wear her costume to the local playground, where my wife and I would always get a kick out of the kids following her all around declaring to their parents, "Mommy, that's Batman!" The parents seemed to wonder about our decision to allow our daughter out of the house and in public with a cape and costume, but the kids on the playground were quick to join her in her quest to rid the playground of all "bad guys." Eventually she discovered Superman, Captain America, Spiderman, and Robin, and in that process her varying masks and capes helped her constantly rotate between superhero identities.

This is normal play for kids, but many adults continue this well into adulthood. They forgo the process of pushing through the anxieties that confront them, and choose instead to settle for an endless rotation of masks that they easily slip on and off so they can retreat into hiding when their fears arise within them.

The word for *mask* comes from the ancient Greek word *prosopon*, meaning "about the eyes," or literally, "face." The mask was a tool the actor used to play a part. By putting on the mask, the actor became another person by vanishing into the face of an acting role. We hide because we live in a culture, especially a Christian culture, that tells us something is wrong with us for experiencing anxiety. Therefore, in our shame, we retreat and hide behind masks and costumes that say, "Hey, look at me, I'm successful. I have everything under control. Life is good." We project this image while underneath we are wrestling with fears, worries, and inadequacies.

Too often as Christians when we experience anxiety we tend to go into hiding, believing that anxiety is not something that Christians should experience. And it is in hiding where shame envelops us. When we feel shame we do everything to mask and cover up the feeling. I believe one of the reasons that so many Christians are afraid to acknowledge their own anxiety, and mask it over by going into hiding, is because they have somehow internalized their feelings of anxiety as being something inherently wrong. They have come to believe the message, "Because I am a Christian and have feelings of anxiety, there must be something wrong with me. As a Christian, I should trust God. And if I really trusted God, I wouldn't be anxious. Therefore, I must not trust God."

Perhaps a pastor may have said something from the pulpit like "there is no place for anxiety in the Christian life because the Bible says don't be anxious." But what happens after the pastor says that and you still have feelings of anxiety? Is something wrong with you?

Or you might have a well-meaning friend who is continually encouraging you to "just let go of your anxiety," but you somehow aren't able to. Are you not a faithful Christian then? Do you just need to spend more time in prayer and daily quiet times, as some may insist?

We send messages all the time to one another as Christians that we intend to be helpful, but if we are not careful, what we end up doing instead is shaming people and driving them into believing that something is wrong with them.

Most of the time these messages are unintended, but there are Christian communities that thrive on shaming one another, hoping that the shame is the catalyst that will produce the change. But it doesn't. It drives people into hiding and isolation, though on the outside they may appear to have it all together. There are Christian communities that fear anxiety because of the freedom of possibility that anxiety opens up before them. They are not comfortable with choice, options, and mystery, and would prefer that someone such as a pastor dictate their life to them from the pulpit.

The anxiety that propels you to freedom is the same anxiety that many in the Christian community prefer that you ignore, and if you don't, then they will convince you that something is wrong with your faith. When we ignore our anxiety it festers and goes to work on how we feel about ourselves—and even worse, on how we perceive God feels about us.

If anxiety can lead us to believe lies about ourselves and about God, then it gains a strong foothold in us and we need to begin the process of defeating those lies and living in the truth.

Coming Out of Hiding

We are not meant to hide, living our lives behind masks. And thankfully we worship a God who does not want us to stay in that place of anxiety and fear. Soon after Adam and

Eve fled in fear from the Lord, we find a most beautiful scene in Genesis 3:21 where He calls them out of hiding and into the light: "The Lord God made garments of skin for Adam and his wife and clothed them." This is a grand demonstration of grace amidst the anxiety of being banished from the garden of Eden and driven into the unknown.

Anxiety has been a part of our human condition from the earliest beginnings. When we experience anxiety we are in that space where a world of freedom and possibility is opened up before us by God. And in that space we have the choice to run and hide, covering up in shame, or we can choose to embrace that anxiety, clothed in grace by God, and allow Him to lead us into freedom and possibility. It is in this place that our lives are transformed.

The choice is yours.

What I am saying about anxiety, and what God is asking of you in your anxiety, is not an easy decision. If it were, then Paul's words in Philippians 4:6, "Do not be anxious about anything," would cure all of our worries. But Paul reminds us in that same letter in Philippians 2:12 that we are to "continue to work out [our] salvation with fear and trembling." There is to be a sense of anxiety as we acknowledge and wrestle with the things that God is wanting for our lives.

Without this anxiety we are creatures who are tempted to play life safe. When we play life safe we are tempted to become content and comfortable, and eventually stagnant. God does not want that of us. To follow after God is to be in a state of heightened alertness and sometimes "knocking knees," as C. S. Lewis put it.

Without our anxiety, we do not become who God desires us to be.

Begin to embrace it on your journey with God.

Discussion Questions

1. How have you most experienced anxiety in your life (i.e., fear, stress, worry, etc.)?

2. When you feel anxious, do you ever find yourself experiencing shame or hiding from others?

3. What are some of the messages that have been communicated to you by the Christian community about anxiety?

Exercises

1. Write down any anxieties that you are currently experiencing.

2. If you feel safe in your group or with someone, share some of these anxieties with another person.

Prayer

God, please take the anxiety that I feel and use it for Your good. Help me to not hide in shame, but instead to be covered by Your grace.

chapter two

Welcoming Uncertainty

"To arrive where you are, to get from where you are not, You must go by a way wherein there is no ecstasy."[1]

T. S. ELIOT, *Four Quartets*

Are you serious? Seriously . . . we are pregnant?"

Those are the words I said to my wife as I looked back and forth from her to the card she had given me before bedtime. I was wondering if somehow I had misunderstood what she wrote. It was in English but I wondered if I had translated those six words "We are going to be parents" incorrectly.

If I can be honest with you, that moment on November 22, 2006, was one of the happiest and most harrowing moments of my life. Those six words opened up the wellspring of anxiety that I had done a great job of sealing off for quite some time. Life moves very rapidly from the announcement to the actual birth. It's a frenzy of activity, filled with decision after decision, and the anxiety continued to rise until it almost became a paralyzing fear for me when I first set foot in a Babies"R"Us.

"What is this place and how do I get out of here," I found myself uttering under my breath.

It was all so very overwhelming.

My wife and I were headed for one of the biggest events in our lives and I just felt unprepared for such a huge change. We were getting used to the married life we were living. We were content. We were comfortable. We enjoyed the freedom of leaving the house whenever we wanted to. We loved going out to late-night dinners together and talking endlessly into the night. We enjoyed sleeping in till 11 a.m. on Saturdays and heading over to Hugo's off Coldwater Canyon and Riverside for early afternoon breakfasts.

We loved our life and we weren't sure how the arrival of a baby would change things. We just knew it would.

In William Bridges's wonderful book *Transitions: Making Sense of Life's Changes*, he says something very powerful about the distinction between change and transition that I have only now begun to understand:

> Our society confuses them constantly, leading us to imagine that transition is just another word for change. But it isn't.... [C]hange is situational. Transition, on the other hand, is psychological. It is not those events, but rather the inner re-orientation and self-redefinition that you have to go through in order to incorporate any of those changes into your life. Without a transition, a change is just a rearrangement of the furniture. Unless transition happens, the change won't work, because it doesn't "take." Whatever

word we use, our society talks a lot about change; but it seldom deals with transition.[2]

We methodically began to plan for the change over the next nine months, but we hadn't adequately begun preparing for the transition that was about to take place. We didn't even know what this transition would look like.

Giving Birth to Change

In the opening chapter of Exodus we find the story of God's people, the Israelites, being oppressed and in slavery to the Egyptians. It's a story that doesn't begin in ideal conditions, but God is not about to abandon His people. Instead, God initiates change in His people's lives through the birth of a baby boy, named Moses, whom He would use to lead His people through the wilderness and toward the Promised Land. This physical journey would also become a psychological one, helping the Israelites transition into the people God was calling them to become. I like that in our biblical story we have the imagery of birth bringing about change and a journey of transition for the people of God. That's a story that resonated with my wife and me as we faced the changes ahead resulting from her pregnancy and the birth of our daughter and the transition into parenthood.

What I find fascinating about the beginning of the Exodus story as well is that it is rooted in a time of anxiety for the Israelites. Not only are they in slavery, in an act of forceful oppression, but the king of Egypt calls all of the Hebrew

41

midwives and orders them to kill any male child that is born to the Israelites. It's a dreadful moment of choice for two Hebrew midwives, Shiphrah and Puah.

They could follow the king's orders, which would ensure weakness and continued slavery for the Israelites, or they could take a stand against the king. To choose to allow the male babies to live is to leave the door open to the possibility of a better future. You can imagine that the decision must have been terrifying. One option was safe, but would kill any hope for change. The other option took tremendous courage, but led to the only hope for freedom.

Anxiety does this.

It arouses the awareness of choice and freedom within us. We have to decide whether we want to face the anxiety, or whether we want to run and hide from it.

Both have their risks.

But we have the choice.

Thankfully for the Israelites, Shiphrah and Puah decided to face their own fears despite their anxiety. In doing so they opened up the possibility for a different future for the people of God, ultimately leading to the birth of Moses. In that moment, God reached down in the midst of chaos, and brought forth the child He had chosen to lead the Israelites out of Egypt. This child Moses would be a man of God who was not only born into a time of cultural anxiety, but who would continue to lead his people, through the wilderness amidst his own fears.

Through the Wilderness

As I was standing at the intersection of a dusty road outside of a remote Honduran village, I was beginning to wonder if my quest to "find myself" was really such a great idea after all. After a long winding boat ride, between the town of Livingston, Guatemala, and my next destination on the island of Roatan, I was standing on that dusty road with two college friends. We were all in our mid-twenties now, and our backpacks once filled with textbooks now contained only the barest of essentials. I was in the midst of a three-and-a-half-month journey living in Antigua, Guatemala, studying Spanish, volunteering in a children's hospital, and trekking by chicken bus through Central America.

I'm not quite sure what it was, but in 2000 at the age of 25, I started to pay more attention to a restless feeling inside of me. Deep down I knew something in my life needed changing. Or perhaps I needed an entirely new direction in life. I was two years into working on my Master of Divinity at Fuller Theological Seminary's extension campus in Phoenix, Arizona, while at the same time working full-time at my alma mater, Grand Canyon University, as a college admission counselor and recruiter. I would spend my days talking to students as they tried to navigate the next big life transition from high school to college, while I spent my nights and weekends buried in my theology textbooks, wrestling with all the difficult questions of life that seminary often thrusts upon someone. All the while I was feeling as lost and restless as the students I counseled and the seminary students I studied alongside of.

I think what the young adults and students had in common was that we had set out on this life journey full of hopes and dreams. But somewhere along the way, our experiences with failure, brokenness, and confusion led to an erosion of the clear path that we all had hoped would lead us to where we were going and wanted to be.

And that left all of us feeling anxious.

That particular stage in life for me—post college to mid-twenties—seemed so limitless with choices, options, and opportunities. It was filled with so many "what ifs." Maybe that's why it felt so scary, so free, and also so paralyzing at times—so anxiety filled.

And then one day while I was reading a passage from the book of Exodus that I had read many times before, a particular text almost seemed to jump off the page, demanding that I give it attention. The text was Exodus 17:1 (NRSV, bold added):

From the **wilderness** of Sin the whole congregation of the **Israelites journeyed by stages**, as the Lord commanded.

As I read that passage, something began to speak deeply within me and I just sat there, transfixed by the text. I was in no rush to continue on with the rest of the passage, but instead I just sat, chewing on the text and meditating on the word "wilderness" and the phrase "journeyed by stages." I have returned to this passage over the last twelve years, and it always reminds me of Eugene Peterson's description of St. John eating the scroll in Revelation 10:9–10:

> St. John, this endlessly fascinating early-church apostle and pastor and writer, walks up to the angel and says, "Give me the book." The angel hands it over, "Here it is; eat it, eat the book." And John does. He eats the book—not just reads it—he got it into his nerve endings, his reflexes, his imagination.[3]

My encounter with the text was not as apocalyptic as St. John's, but it was life transforming nonetheless. That passage in Exodus went "into my nerve endings," into my "reflexes," and has continued to shape my imagination and guide me along this journey.

Exodus 17:1 continually reminds me that we are people in the wilderness. There is just no way around it. The reality of life is that we are constantly moving from one big transition to another. At moments we may experience a respite from the journey, but that doesn't alter the fact that life is rooted in the wilderness experience of continuous transition and choice.

One of the reasons we experience anxiety is that God is persistently trying to move us through the wilderness, because it is in that wilderness that we are most dependent upon Him. It is in that wilderness experience that God shapes us into the people He desires us to become. I believe this was largely the motivating factor for my move from Scottsdale, Arizona, to Antigua, Guatemala, at twenty-six. I was stuck and the anxiety I felt was God prompting me to get unstuck and to get going.

I had gotten pretty good at doing life all by myself. I had a college degree, a good job, great friends, and I was living on my own. I was independent, which after all is what most college graduates want for themselves. Or at least their parents do. I was in my mid-twenties, beginning to feel more confident about who I was and of God's working in my life, especially with my stuttering. I was no longer living in that anxious fear of talking and speaking in class or at work. But I felt like something was missing. I felt like God was not content to leave me where I was at, but wanted much more for my life. I needed something to change. I needed to take a risk and put myself out there. I wanted to put myself in a place where I was less self-dependent, and more God-dependent. And in my move to Central America I experienced a variety of challenging circumstances. I was radically confronted with a wide array of cultural, political, and theological differences. In those times when my anxiety was most acute I began to lean more heavily upon God to lead me through.

In a time when our self-sufficiency and the usual tools we rely on to get us through begin to disappear, and the security we once felt begins to evade us, we start to feel off-balance. My experience in Guatemala was just that. It was a time of intentional disorientation for me as I knew that the unsettled feeling would demand nothing less from me than to take a risk and venture forth into an unknown future. My anxiety pushed me forward, and God prompted it.

Wandering through unknown territory is disorienting and uncomfortable, but that is the reality of this aspect of any journey. It's the point where we have left our safe spot, but haven't yet reached the next destination. Our tendency is to try to bypass the wilderness or to skip over it as much as possible, but it is in exactly that place where we are shaped and transformed. The Old Testament scholar Walter Brueggemann frames this journey as a movement from orientation to disorientation to new orientation.[4] But in order for us to arrive at a new orientation, at a new place in life that God is calling us toward, we must first venture out of what we know (orientation),[5] and take the risk to head into what we don't know (disorientation).[6] It is then, and only then, in that state of anxiety and disorientation that we are in the place to receive the new life (new orientation)[7] that God so strongly desires for us.

We don't like to be in the wilderness, but if we try to rush it we cheat ourselves out of what God is doing in our lives. Brueggemann puts it eloquently when he states:

> The dominant ideology of our culture is committed to continuity and success and to the avoidance of pain, hurt, and loss. The dominant culture is also resistant to genuine newness and real surprise. It is curious but true, that surprise is as unwelcome as is loss. And our culture is organized to prevent the experience of both.[8]

We all come to a time and place in our lives when we find ourselves in the midst of the wilderness, either by intention or accident. Maybe anxiety prompted you to start a journey, to take a risk, or maybe anxiety is causing you unrest in this spot.

God is at work.

Journeying by Stages

When God calls us through the wilderness He leads us on a stage-by-stage journey. I did not understand this part of the text until recent years when I really began to embrace this journey in my own life. God does not call you into the wilderness and move you in one simple movement from *A* to *Z*, from beginning to end. Rather, He leads you on a journey through the wilderness step by step and stage by stage where "every step [is] arrival."[9]

God leads us from one place to another and at times He camps us for a period of time in a certain spot. It may be for a day. It may be for weeks. It may be for months at a time. It may even be for years. Our tendency is to move quickly from place to place in order to avoid the feeling of disorientation, but that is not how God seems to work. There are things He desires to teach us in those places where He camps us along the journey. New Testament scholar Robert Guelich and writer Janet Hagberg describe this process in their excellent book *The Critical Journey*: "For those who choose to take the journey, it is lifelong. The longer the journey, the more nuances it takes on and the more it opens up to broader experiences. Yet, a journey must progress step by step. So it is with our spiritual journey."[10]

In these places we eagerly wait for God to do something. But when we realize that God is not in a hurry and we are, our anxiety begins to stir within us. The physical distance of the Israelites' journey from the slavery of Egypt into the freedom of the Promised Land should have taken thirteen days.

But instead their journey lasted forty difficult years.

Why did God leave them on the journey for so long?

Why does God choose to lead us on the journey we are on?

God is a God who moves His people on a journey, bit by bit and step by step. Take notice of the movement described in Numbers 33:1–2: "These are the stages by which the Israelites went out of the land of Egypt in military formation under the leadership of Moses and Aaron. Moses wrote down their starting points, stage by stage, by command of the Lord; and these are their stages according to their starting places" (NRSV).

In these first two verses alone we get the sense of a journey by stages. As we continue reading we discover a movement of people led by God through the wilderness, where forty-one times in the span of forty-nine verses we see that they "left and camped."

"Left and camped . . . left and camped . . . left and camped."

Forty-one times they leave where they are at.

And forty-one times they come to camp at a new place.

That is a lot of change. A lot of transition. A lot of disorientation.

You can imagine that this type of movement produces a lot of anxiety.

It is in those in-between spaces of time that the fear of the unknown and the instability of our situation begin to creep into our minds in the form of anxiety. We would prefer that God would just do what He needed to do and take us from where we are to where we need to be. We don't want to drag out the change and the transition, nor do we want the anxiety that accompanies this type of journey. We just want God to initiate the change and complete the transition for us in one easy step.

But it is exactly in those in-between spaces of time—where our anxiety is most acute—that God shapes us into the people He wants us to become. It is in these times that we should strive to learn what He is trying to teach us.

What I didn't say at the outset of the chapter was that the news of our pregnancy was the anxiety that God used to really encourage Heather and me to reimagine how we wanted to live our lives. And more importantly, how we believed God wanted us to live our lives. It was the scary and wonderful news of a baby and the accompanying anxiety that drove us deep into conversation where we wrestled through what God wanted of us.

I love God's timing.

The day after finding out we were pregnant we were driving across the desert wilderness from California to Arizona for Thanksgiving with my parents in Scottsdale. In a newly disoriented state my wife and I began to talk about the stage of life that God had us in, and where we believed He was calling us. At some point during that journey across the desert I began playing a podcast I had recorded before our trip and wanted to listen to along the way. I fully expected my wife to doze off like she usually did after a few minutes on a road trip, but that didn't happen.

What happened was that we were both captured by the words of writer Donald Miller as he preached at Mars Hill

Church in Michigan. In the sermon Miller began to talk about the concept of story as a metaphor for how we live our lives. And my wife and I both remember being mesmerized by a question that Miller asked that day.

"Are you living a good story?" he asked.

Heather and I looked at each other, but we didn't know how to answer that question.

We were happy. We were expecting a baby. We made a good double-income. We had great friends. We owned a beautiful house in Pasadena, California. We had a great church community. We loved our work. We had all these things, but we wondered if our lives indicated that we were living a good story? Were people compelled by our story? Did God think we were living a good story?

Our inability to answer these questions to our satisfaction left us both with a feeling of anxiousness as we realized that we might be living a good story according to most people, but we weren't living the story God wanted us to live. We knew that the anxiety stirring in our hearts was God calling us to live a better story than what we were living. Like the Exodus story that begins in anxiety and the pregnancy and birthing pains of a people of God, our story was now filled with anxiety as we found ourselves pregnant, and anxiously awaiting the birth of a new baby. It was the catalyst that propelled us to begin the movement out of our current stage in life's journey and into a new stage of disorientation.

By the time we entered the sprawling western suburbs of Phoenix we had made up our minds that we would set in motion a plan to move from Los Angeles to Dallas. After the birth of our daughter, Heather and I decided that we wanted to be closer to family for support, so Dallas seemed like a good option since my in-laws were in the Dallas-Fort Worth area and I had relatives there as well. There was also an inner peace that moving to Texas would be a bit of a homecoming for our family since I had been born in Odessa, Texas, and a move to Dallas felt almost like we were coming full circle. My mom had also been a Texan through and through, and just being in the state made me feel a close connection to her that I hadn't had since her death. The move would not happen till August of 2008, and the transition that came from that change is still in progress today. But we never would have gotten here if it weren't for the anxiety created by the question Miller asked, and our lack of satisfaction with the answers we could produce.

Stuck at "What if?"

The in-between stage on this journey through life is a scary place. To be caught between the comfort and security of the life we know and the disarray of what lies ahead can fill us with anxiety. If we are honest, most of us do not want to step out and make the necessary changes to move through a new transition in life, even if we believe God is prompting us to.

Sometimes the changes choose us and sometimes we choose them. Whether we choose the change or not, there are stages of life before us that cannot be avoided and that will plunge us into instability and confusion whether we are ready or not. That is just the reality of life.

You have a choice though in these matters.

Listen to your anxiety, for it may be God prompting you to enter that period of disorientation so that He can shape you to become the person He wants you to be.

Maybe the whispering you hear is God saying, "Step out, take a risk. Trust Me. I know it's scary, but trust Me." Or if you are already in that place of disorientation, listen to your anxiety, for it may also be God calling you down a path and into a new life that is awaiting you. Maybe that still quiet voice is saying, "Turn this way, not that way. Go this direction, not that direction. Be quiet. Sit still. Okay, move forward."

Most of us get stuck at some stage in life. We get stuck trying to make the leap into it or find ourselves stuck in the midst of it. We live in constant fear of making the wrong decision or choosing the wrong path. But as the writer Scott Peck reminds us, it's in our times of discomfort that we often gain the greatest insights:

> The truth is that our finest moments are most likely to occur when we are feeling deeply uncomfortable, unhappy, or unfulfilled. For it is only in such moments, propelled by our discomfort, that we are likely to step out of our ruts and start searching for different ways or truer answers.[11]

We wrestle through a lot of "what ifs" in the journey of following God. Most young adults face an onslaught of choices and decisions. *What if I choose the wrong college? What if I take the wrong job? What if I marry the wrong person? What if I'm not cut out to be a good parent? What if I'm not happy?*

These questions are full of fear, but these are fears that you must face if you are ever to move forward and not get stuck in an unhealthy spiral of fear and doubt.

On July 14, 2007, my anxiety had reached an all-time high as I wondered, "What if I'm not going to be a good enough dad?" I had just seen my daughter's beautiful face for the first time. It was a moment of tremendous change for us, and the beginning of a lifetime of transition. It is hard to find a more disorienting moment than being in the delivery room. My wife was in a lot of pain, we were functioning on little sleep, and my anxiety was kicking around my stomach like rampaging bulls running down the streets of Pamplona, Spain.

But had my wife and I not been willing to face the "what ifs" and leave the comfortable and secure life we were living, we would never have been able to experience the completely disorienting and life-giving journey of following God where He was leading us. And now that we have come through part of our journey we are beginning to see the fruition of new life that awaits us because we were willing to face our fears and follow God. Whether it was pregnancy and labor, or packing up moving vans and changing careers, our willingness to face that anxiety has been a process by which we have seen God really grow us as individuals and as a couple.

In facing the fears that come along with all of your "what ifs," you are allowing anxiety to propel you out of your place of comfort so that you may enter into the temporary place of disorientation where God will shape you in ways that you never could have imagined.

Discussion Questions

1. What transition in your life has produced the most anxiety? How did you deal with that anxiety?

2. What stage in your journey do you believe God has you in?

3. What are some of your "what if" questions that are producing a lot of anxiety for you?

Exercise

Create your life line.[12]

- On a blank sheet of paper, draw a line to represent your life. This line may have ups and downs, go back and forth, wander around in circles, be jagged, curved, etc. You are creating a representation of your life.

- At points along your line, place notations that represent significant events, changes, and experiences, or encounters with God or other people who have altered or shaped the direction of your life.

- You might want to draw symbols at significant points along your line such as a plant for growth, a tombstone for the loss of someone close, a rain cloud for a sad time, sunshine for a happy time—creativity is encouraged.

- Now place an X at the end of your line to represent where you are now in your life.

- Look back over your line and reflect on your life's directions, dimensions, turning points. Make note of the feelings you have as you reflect back on your life.

Also, take note of anything you might want to say to God about what you see in your life, especially the times when you experienced anxiety. Think about ways God may have been at work in your life during these anxious times.

• Continue on from the *X* with a dotted line to indicate where you would desire your life to go. Take a few moments to talk with God about this future direction.

• Take some time to share your life line with at least one other person.

Prayer

As I find myself in that in-between place of my present reality and my unknown future, I ask, Lord, that You would lead me through the wilderness. I ask that You take those anxious events that have negatively shaped my past and that You help me see Your presence in the midst of them.

chapter three

Stuck in a Rut

"These kinds of experiences are not biodegradable. They float in the reservoir of memory forever." [1]

IAN CRON, *Jesus, My Father, the CIA, and Me*

I remember my dad picking up the phone receiver on about the second ring that early Sunday morning.

It was around 3:30 a.m., and growing up in the home of a pastor I was accustomed to late-night calls. But late-night calls never brought good news, and this one in particular left me with a feeling of anxiety deep inside my heart as my stomach bunched up in knots. I heard my dad exchange a few words on the phone, telling the caller he would be there right away.

As my dad dressed and headed out the door I was in that semidelirious state between wakefulness and sleep. But I was conscious enough to know that things were going to be a lot different when I awoke that morning.

My dad returned to our home sometime around 6:30 a.m. and came over to sit in bed with my brother and me who were still sleeping.

I knew what was coming before my dad even said the

words, but nothing can prepare you for such news.

"Your mom has passed away."

All that anxiety that I had been living with for years, each anxious day where I was left wondering if this would be the day my mom would finally die as the doctors had been predicting for so long—that day was here.

Though I don't remember the exact words that were said, I do remember the painful struggle that morning. My dad told my brother and me that he wanted to take us up to the hospital to see my mom one last time. In the midst of all the tears, frustration, confusion, and fears, I do remember one thing very vividly coming from my father's mouth.

"You won't understand this now, but you will be thankful later that I took you to see your mom."

There is no blueprint in life for how to deal with the death of a loved one, for life does not go according to one's plans when a family member is dying of breast cancer. But my dad's insistence on us seeing her is one thing that I have come to appreciate more and more with each passing day since her death.

But the anxiety leading to that moment was unbearable.

My brother and I dressed, got into the car with my dad, and cried all the way to the hospital, pleading if there could be any other possible way to do this.

This was perhaps the first time in my life that I had to directly face my own overwhelming anxiety.

We walked into the Good Samaritan Hospital, entered the elevator, and walked down the hallways of the fourth floor. My brother and I knew this place well. This hospital had become our second home as we had spent so much time there. Most of the beginning of my fifth-grade year seemed to be spent hanging out there after school, studying and talking with my mom as she lay in her hospital bed. The nurses, the rooms, the halls, and all the smells were very familiar to us.

But today was different.

Nothing seemed familiar.

It was very quiet in the hall.

All the faces of the nurses I knew looked expressionless, not knowing how to convey the sadness that they were feeling as we slowly walked by them.

And as we walked toward her corner room where I knew she now lay dead, I had no more ideas or understanding of what life would now look like for me.

Upon crossing the threshold we entered a very peaceful scene as my grandfather (who had already lost his mother, his wife, and now his oldest daughter to breast cancer; and in 2001 would lose his youngest daughter to the disease as well), other relatives, and close friends were there in the room with her.

All I wanted to do was get out of there as quickly as possible.

I remember sitting next to my mom on the bed, touching her lifeless hand, as someone (probably my dad) explained to me that it was no longer Melodee there in that cancer-ridden body, but that she was now with the Lord and at peace. I knew that was true, but it can be almost impossible to reconcile with the truth during times of crisis. God can feel so distant. All I wanted was for her to be here with me.

It's amazing to me how powerful those memories of April 20, 1986, still are. I can sometimes feel the anxiety of that time even now.

Forming a Well-Worn Rut

When my wife and I were first married we purchased a house in Pasadena, California. We loved the neighborhood. And what I loved most was being able to walk outside our home and stare up at the San Gabriel Mountains about one mile north of us.

I enjoyed putting on my running shoes, heading out the door, and running toward those mountain trails that had been worn underfoot over the years. There were miles and miles of trails and varying switchbacks I could choose to run on each day. Some days I chose to do a little more exploring and venture off onto my own trail that had not been worn down by other runners, but most of the time I liked the ease of running up and down trails that were smooth from all of the foot traffic over the years.

Some of these trails became ravines during the rainy season or when the occasional snow would melt. The water would head down the path of least resistance and over the smooth running trails, rather than the more difficult route through dirt and rocks and brush that presented greater obstacles.

Over time we too begin to form trails and paths among the complex wiring of our brains. As we go through life and encounter certain experiences, our brain receives those signals and begins to make sense of them and respond accordingly. Over time we begin to wire our brain in such a way that whenever we experience feeling *A*, for example, we respond with behavior *B*. A pattern is soon formed between our feelings and coping behaviors that becomes very familiar to us. So familiar that it becomes an easy and automatic response. In essence, the more that we experience feeling *A*, and respond with behavior *B*, the more worn and trod this pathway in our brain becomes.

According to recent brain studies, we are literally stuck in a rut:[2]

> As a result, we choose our most instinctual coping behavior when certain feelings arise. We often choose this path because it is also the direction that confronts us with the least anxiety.

When presented with a path, which one would you choose?

The path that has been worn down, feels safe and natural, and allows you to avoid anxiety?

Or the path that is rough, hard to navigate, and that causes fear to well up inside of you?

If given the option, most of us would choose the path that is more habitual for us and feels like home. We tell ourselves that the path of least resistance is the greatest opportunity for us not to fail, and the best chance for us to avoid feeling uncomfortable or afraid in the process.

The problem is that eventually we must face our anxiety if

we are to grow and thrive as God's created beings. But anxiety becomes harder to face the longer we continue down the rutted paths in our lives. Well-worn paths that have been trampled underfoot are great to ease the running experience, but they provide little opportunity for a runner to grow new muscle and develop new navigational skills. Our well-worn ruts may allow us to easily navigate through life, but they provide little opportunity for us to be challenged, face risk, and grow in the process.

Each day we confront choices that can either help us grow or that just keep us on the same well-worn path, stuck in a status-quo groove. There is nothing inherently wrong with choosing the same path over and over again, except that you are going to end up in the same place again and again. The path you choose can have great influence on where you end up. As poet Robert Frost described it:

> Two roads diverged in a wood, and I took the one less traveled by, and that has made all the difference.[3]

Family Matters

There are few contexts as vital in shaping who we become as our families. Our families, for good or bad, provide the context that not only informs us of who we are, but shapes us through the environment and experiences we have with them.

Our lives are like a living, breathing garden that when properly attended to by our family, has the opportunity to flourish and bloom. But if neglected and abused, it can wilt and die.

Some of us look at our families and feel very fortunate and blessed. We believe that they did a pretty good job of raising us. They created a home that fostered an environment of love and trust,[4] and there was a sense of feeling secure and knowing that we were wanted as we grew up in that home.

Some of us look around at our families and we can't find much that we are thankful for, and we feel that we have somehow been cheated out of what we were entitled[5] to as children growing up in a family. We look around at our friends and long for parents and relatives who could provide what theirs do. We don't feel secure and we often question whether or not we are really wanted.

Whichever best describes your family life, the reality is that our families and the experiences we have had with them have powerfully shaped us, leaving an indelible mark upon our lives.

The way that you and I responded to our anxiety (fight-or-flight) as children, which was significantly shaped by our families' influence, set in us early on a pattern of coping that over the years has essentially been hardwired into our brains, and is now the automatic response that we give whenever anxiety is present. But very few of us are aware of this.

Learning from the Past

I initially began seeing a therapist at the age of twenty-three because I was noticing that I was anxious and having a hard time making choices with a strong sense of conviction. Instead, my decisions were filled with lots of doubt as I always wondered "what if." This anxiety also affected my ability to maintain healthy relationships with girlfriends. I knew that somehow my family experience, and more specifically the early loss of my mother to breast cancer, held an important clue to what I was feeling and how I was behaving.

This was just the beginning of really understanding how important my early experiences were with my family and other key figures in my life in shaping who I became. But my work was not done.

I returned to therapy at the age of thirty with my fiancée, Heather, so that we could do our premarital work prior to our marriage. More clues began to emerge as our therapist really helped us understand that how we felt and behaved toward one another in our relationship was greatly influenced by both our positive and negative experiences with our families of origin. We were told that marriage was often the place that we work out our family of origin issues.

As more and more clues began to emerge in my personal therapy work, I entered the marriage and family therapy program (MSMFT) at Fuller Theological Seminary. The program was more of an endeavor to make me a better college pastor so that I could be equipped to really help students through many of the issues they were experiencing. But it was also a return to one of my early dreams to be a therapist as well. As it turned out, this experience was not just about helping others, but the program began the process of really helping me understand who I was and how anxiety was inhabiting such a large space in my life.

Early on in the program I was doing my family of origin work with the assistance of a genogram,[6] which is an illustrated family tree that displays information about the relationships that are listed. Although I finished that genogram assignment out of requirement, I became more and more curious about what I had discovered in the process. That curiosity led me to eventually spend almost every week for the next two and a half years going to therapy just so I could unpack all that I was discovering about myself.

Looking back at our families of origin and remembering these details can be a scary process for many people. Sometimes we are not quite sure what we will discover or remember, and that can leave us feeling anxious. That is normal. When we look back, and really try to sort through our relationships and experiences with our family, the intention is not to place blame or punish others. One of the things that keeps many people stuck in life is their fear of looking back. They surmise that, "Hey, the past is the past; don't dwell on it." It just seems easier to forget.

But if we fear looking back at the past, or downplay how the past has shaped us, we may never really learn who we are and how we have been wired. Our past is important for each of us because in the words of novelist Chaim Potok's character Asher Lev, "My frames of reference have been formed by the life I have lived."[7]

Once we begin to see the patterns and how those interactions shaped who we are today, it provides a powerful opportunity for us to begin to understand ourselves better. In that awareness we are then freed to begin to make the changes we want in life. Without awareness and knowledge of who we are and how we were shaped in our family of origin, there is little motivation and opportunity to change the way we have always operated.

Looking back provides us with the opportunity to review the past because the past is important. The past has shaped who we are presently, has a profound influence on how we react in times of fear or pain, and will continue to shape who we will be in the future. The Bible speaks to the importance of remembering the past in both the Old and New Testaments, with the words in the original languages communicating several related meanings.

They call us to *"remember."*

They call us to *"bring to mind."*

They call us to *"make present."*

They call us to *"make alive."*

I love what pastor and writer Drew Sams says in his incredible work "The Re-Membered Church":

When we remember who God is and who God created us to be, then God re-members the broken fragments of our lives into something whole and beautiful. Furthermore, in order for the community of God's people to be whole in its identity, it must remember the whole of God's Story as revealed thrugh the biblical narrative, rather than just fragments of it.[8]

As we look back at our families of origin and how they shaped us, we practice the biblical concept of remembering, and in doing so we can participate in the reshaping of who God has created us to be. But it's important that we remember the whole story—what our experience was like, how we felt in those moments, and what messages we received from our families.

By participating in the process of remembering we are given the task to take responsibility for our lives. Too many people look back at the past and fall prey to becoming a passive victim who shirks responsibility and in the process forfeits their opportunity to reshape their present and future with God. It's important to understand how you became who you are today, but equally important to ask yourself who you want to be. Pastor and counselor Howard Stone puts it eloquently as he comments on this idea from the writings of Kierkegaard:

> Possibility addresses the future. It is what we can become as we use our freedom. In that respect our possibilities are not predetermined. We are not automatons. We can imagine, and within the givens of life we can become something new. Living as an authentic self . . . means looking beyond our immediate necessities or past liabilities. We anticipate the future with the awareness that we are free—however limited—to actualize whom we ought to become as faithful Christians and to take responsibility for shaping that future.[9]

The Anxious Christian

Finally, this process also allows us the opportunity to exercise grace to ourselves and to others. As we muster up the courage to face our past, we may be surprised to realize that we weren't the only ones having a difficult time in life and struggling to make it day to day. As we review the past and take responsibility for our lives, we may begin to slowly realize that often our parents were doing the best they could. Maybe what you got from them was all they knew how to give. This is not to excuse areas in your life where parents should have been more present, more encouraging, less critical, etc. But maybe that knowledge may free you up enough to let go and live in freedom from the bondage of the past.

Charting Family History

For years I had been trying to fully understand the root of my anxiety and stuttering. But it became much clearer when I was able to see my family history on a page. Charting my genogram allowed my family history to come alive and I began to see the myriad of ways that breast cancer had impacted generations of our family, and how those experiences not only shaped our relating to one another, but produced lots of anxiety.

As I began to take a closer look at my family, several very distinct things became clear to me that helped me begin to better understand who I was. I began to notice the numerous deaths of family members that I had been very close to. And even beyond that I began to really see how many important female "mother type" figures in my life had died of breast cancer. I had known this, but to see it in front of me on a piece of paper had a penetrating way of illuminating it like never before.

As I looked at my genogram and noticed those circles indicating females, coupled with Xs through them indicating death, a family pattern began to emerge that slowly helped me better name and understand the emotions and behaviors that I had been living with for more than twenty-five years. I began to see that my childhood and adult life had been greatly impacted by breast cancer, and loss, creating a chaotic world of anxiety where I felt out of control, abandoned, and alone.

Although feelings of abandonment began early for me, I wasn't really aware of it until I began to look back, remember, and connect the experiences by looking at the bigger picture.

It began with the loss of my grandmother to breast cancer in 1984 and was greatly accelerated with the constant fear of losing my mom to breast cancer from the time she was diagnosed in 1981 until her death in 1986. My mom's death left a huge hole in my life and that feeling of abandonment created unhealthy behaviors. I began to withdraw and shut down, hoping that someone would pursue me and not abandon me. I needed others to let me know that I was wanted and wouldn't be left alone.

This pattern of feeling out of control/abandoned/alone and coping by withdrawal/shutdown/passive-aggressive behavior became more and more of an automatic and instinctual part of my life. It was the rut that was forming early on and the one I was beginning to tread most of the time. It was this old pattern of functioning that I knew best, and it wasn't going to die easily. Terry Hargrave and Franz Pfitzer make this statement regarding our "old ideas":

> What we know through the field of neuroscience is that old ideas die hard because the brain holds on to those functions in an automatic fashion. Once the brain has learned certain thoughts and behaviors, it is tenacious in holding on to them and, indeed, actually prefers the old behaviors to new learning.[10]

There were times when I was slightly aware of my negative patterns of behavior, but just when I would muster the courage to try to face my anxiety and make positive changes, it was as if I was being punched in the face again and again, and I felt God just stood silent on the sidelines.

In the fall of 1997 my dad's remarriage ended in divorce.

More feelings of abandonment ensued, which led to more withdrawal.

And just when I finally thought I couldn't be abandoned any further, my aunt who was earlier diagnosed with breast cancer and had become a second mother to me, passed away on February 6, 2001. Though no one had intentionally done anything to me, I once again felt abandoned. When people disappear out of your life either through death or divorce it can create a variety of feelings, but I just felt alone and abandoned.

With each loss, anxiety and fear were close at hand, grinding me deeper and deeper into that rut.

Ian Cron in his book *Jesus, My Father, the CIA, and Me*

puts it poignantly when he writes, "The conviction that I was an unlovable freak had metastasized in my heart so that I curved in on myself."[11]

I was beginning to believe the conviction in my heart that I was alone and abandoned, and anxiety forced me to cave in on myself in the form of more withdrawal and passive-aggressive behavior.

Discussion Questions

1. As you look back at your family of origin, what are one or two experiences that have really shaped who you are today? How?

2. Thinking about some of your experiences growing up that shaped who you are:

   a) What feelings/emotions did you experience in those situations?

   b) Whenever you experienced those feelings/emotions, how did you tend to behave? What did you do? What was your coping behavior?[12]

3. What cycle of negative feelings and coping behaviors (pain cycle) has become a rut for you?

Exercise

Develop a family genogram as a tool that will help assist you in your reflecting back on the past. For helpful instructions, see http://genogram.freeservers.com/.

Software for creating genograms is also available at
www.genopro.com.

Prayer

*God, I pray that I can surrender to You any negative
ways that have shaped me. And in Your grace I pray that
You will give me the courage to face my freedom and
reshape my future with You.*

chapter four

Anxiety Reimagined

"Anxiety is the dizziness of freedom."[1]

SØREN KIERKEGAARD, *The Concept of Anxiety*

As I struggled with my anxiety while living in Guatemala I began to notice that my feelings were similar to much of the culture I was now living in. We were right in the middle of the Lenten season and anxiety filled the air as weekly processions of floats constructed out of flowers paraded through the narrow cobblestone streets of Antigua. The journey of Lent is remembrance of suffering that leads to death, in anticipation of a resurrection that brings about new life.

As an American I realized very quickly how foreign it was for me to be still during a season of remembering suffering and death. I knew the story of Easter and how it ended, so I tended to rush to the ending, hoping to avoid the feelings that accompany such a heart-wrenching component of our Christian faith.

For most of my life I sped through the story, going straight to the resurrection and what awaited me on the other side. It was not until my great friend Neil Gatten, a Lutheran youth pastor, invited me to my first ever Ash Wednesday service in Scottsdale, Arizona, that I was introduced to the beauty of the Lenten season for the first time. It's crazy to think that at the age of twenty-six such a fundamental component of my faith had been absent.

By speeding through the story, I was missing a critical piece of God's Story and how He chose to tell it. I was learning a very important lesson from my friends and the Guatemalans who participated in Lent. Suffering and death need to be a central component of the Easter journey. There cannot be a resurrection, and out of that new life, without having gone through a journey of suffering and death. This is a paradox that is fundamental to our faith as Christians, and is crucial for us to understand if we are going to be able to move out of positions of fear and insecurity and into the bold new life that God is calling us to embrace.

There cannot be new life without embracing and moving through the pain and suffering, and allowing God to reshape it into something beautiful.

Reimagining New Life

When Christ was crucified on that bleak Friday afternoon in 33 A.D. it was a crushing blow to all of His followers, especially His disciples who had been living in fearful anticipation. The disciples held hopes that Christ was going to usher in a very powerful reign and that they would play an integral role in it. But in His death all of their hopes and dreams of what they envisioned for their lives vanished, drowned out by the hammering of spikes into His body. It was a frenzied scene as the disciples, caught up in their own anxiety and fear, fled for the nearest place to hide (John 20:19). As N. T. Wright points out:

> When Jesus was crucified, every single disciple knew what it meant: we backed the wrong horse. The game is over. Whatever their expectations, and however Jesus had been trying to redefine those expectations, as far as they were concerned hope had crumbled into ashes. They knew they were lucky to escape with their own lives. . . . That is the world within which early Christianity burst upon the scene as a new thing, and yet not new.[2]

We are much more like the disciples than we would care to admit. We cling to Christ when things are going well, but we are quick to scurry into hiding when we become anxious and fear begins to penetrate every part of our being. Like the disciples, we too are then filled with worry and doubt, wondering about all the promises represented by Christ and His kingdom.

Our anxiety betrays the frail and human condition of our beliefs and behaviors as we struggle to follow after God when things in our life aren't going as we had planned.

When you find yourself in despair, down in the pits wondering who will rescue you, it is hard to reimagine new life coming out of that place. When you find yourself full of fear, paralyzed to make any decisions, worried that your choice will lead you in the wrong direction, it is hard to reimagine new life from that vantage point.

But new life awaits you in the midst of your anxiety-filled journey.

It was not the end of life that dark Friday afternoon when the disciples' hopes of a Christ who would be king came crashing down. Although they did not realize it, it was just the beginning of new life for them and for all of us as His followers. God was about to reshape their pain and suffering into something they could not have imagined.

On those dark days, when you are deep in despair and you don't know where to go or what to do, remember, it is not the end.

That is the turning point to new life.

God does not leave you alone in your anxiety, but uses it to awaken you and help turn you toward Him. It is God's tool to help you grow, and the catalyst that helps us get unstuck and move out of the rut. God places anxiety within you as a way for you to give birth to new life and to follow after the new opportunities that are out there that He is calling you toward.

If you are currently struggling with anxiety, or have been struggling with it for most of your life, then that may be hard for you to reimagine. It may be hard for you to believe that God would take that anxiety that has caused you so much pain and actually use it as a way to help you grow.

If you are struggling with this idea of reimagining anxiety, that is okay.

You are in good company.

Like the disciples of Christ, whose dreams were shattered at His crucifixion, it can be hard to then reimagine new life. But the resurrection allows us to reimagine a new life and a new way of living that we have always thought impossible.

Resurrection is the promise of new life out of death. It is the hope that we hang on to in a chaotic and anxious world. Eugene Peterson reminds us that "The resurrection of Jesus establishes the entire Christian life in the action of God by the Holy Spirit. The Christian life begins as a community that is gathered at the place of impossibility, the tomb."[3]

When I was a seminary student studying New Testament, we were assigned to do an exegetical paper on 1 Corinthians 15. As I worked over a period of a few months I slowly began to be transformed by what the apostle Paul says in verses 12–14:

> Now if Christ is proclaimed as raised from the dead, how can some of you say there is no resurrection of the dead? If there is no resurrection of the dead, then Christ has not been raised; and if Christ has not been raised, then our proclamation has been in vain and your faith has been in vain. (NRSV)

It seemed to me that these few verses boiled down all of the Bible and all of my theology to their most fundamental core: that if there is no resurrection of the dead, then Christ has not been raised. And, therefore, all my teaching, speaking, counseling, belief in Him, and what the Bible teaches has been useless. The resurrection is fundamental to the rest of the story.

As I pored over the text more and more those few months, I learned that the Greek word for resurrection, *anastasis*, is used forty-two times in the New Testament. It's a crucial word in the context of Paul's writing to the people in Corinth, where it is used four times in 1 Corinthians 15. *Anastasis* is an especially important word in this chapter because the crux of Paul's argument is built upon its use in this passage.

On that Easter Sunday when Christ was resurrected everything changed for us. So then why do so many of us live as if Christ has not been resurrected? Why do so many of us live in death, choosing not to have the new life that He promises? Unless I believe that out of Christ's death and resurrection came new life, then what am I living for?

God took something that was not supposed to be—life out of death—and made it a reality for you and me.

I love how God worked in the midst of all their anxiety and fear of death, using what the people knew to be true based on the reality of their experience. No one returns from the dead.

Like everyone else who has ever lived, the disciples knew that dead men did not rise from the grave. But God flipped that truth on its head and they became witnesses to death transforming into life as Christ was raised from the tomb on that anxious and joy-filled Easter morning.

The disciples on that Good Friday were not prepared for the reimagining that Sunday's resurrection would demand of them. On that Good Friday when Christ was crucified, all of the dreams of those who had placed their hopes in Him died right before their eyes. We have the luxury of hindsight that frees us from the anxiety that the disciples felt on that fateful day. But that day was just the beginning of reimagining what resurrection would mean when Christ entered into death and emerged into new life on the third day.

We have the opportunity as well to reimagine what the anxiety in our lives means for us and how it can be used. When we choose to not face our anxieties we participate in the dying of the dreams and passions that God has birthed in us. By doing so we allow anxiety to lead us into bondage and death, rather than into freedom and life.

I choose to believe Christ died and was resurrected to new life. That's the hope I was hanging on to that Easter morning of 1996 when I preached to my fellow college students. It is the same hope that gives me confidence that though my mom died on April 20, 1986, she was raised to new life. She was resurrected.

Reimagining Our Anxiety

In June of 2002 I found myself sitting upstairs in the college intern's office at Bel Air Presbyterian Church in Los Angeles. I had been interning there since September of 2001 and I was just trying to bide my time so that I could complete the nine-month church internship that Fuller Seminary requires of all of its Master of Divinity students. I just wanted to finish that internship, get my degree, and move on to a PhD program where I could lock myself away among my books in a quiet library. I didn't realize it then, but that desire to become a professor and a writer was my safe rut, a route that would allow me to avoid the risk of ever having to publicly preach again. Somehow I forgot that professors have to get up and speak in front of others. If I could avoid having to ever preach or speak in public again, then I could avoid the humiliating embarrassment I felt when I began to stutter in front of others.

I was swiveling back and forth in my chair looking out the second-story office window at the Getty Museum in the distance. It seemed apropos that as I was gazing at the museum out the window, I was at the same time pondering my future, like one who stares at a famous painting for hours at a time looking for any and every little bit of meaning. I had only wanted to come and do my internship as quietly and quickly as possible, but now I was looking at a job offer to become the new college director at Bel Air Presbyterian Church. This was one of those pivotal moments in my life where I found myself facing a fork in the road. My anxiety was bubbling over as I wondered what the right decision should be for me.

What if I made the wrong choice? What if I took this job, but was supposed to pursue a PhD? What if I took this job and failed? What if I couldn't get into a PhD program?

Lots and lots of decisions to make.

At many points in our life we come to a place of transition where we must choose between paths. It's a moment of anxiety and risk because we are not guaranteed any certainty in our decisions, nor are we granted a risk-free passage along the journey.

I knew for certain that if I took the college director position I would be forced to live with the fear of preaching a sermon every week, constantly dealing with the anguish of having to actually get up there and deliver it. This I knew for certain. I could palpably feel that anxiety in my stomach as I sat in that chair, and I hadn't even made a decision yet.

I also knew for certain that choosing to turn down the job would be stressful as I would be faced with the decision of what to do next and where to go as my graduation date was quickly approaching.

But being free means choosing to face our fears and confront our anxiety directly. For everything we say yes to, there are a host of other things we must say no to. We cannot have it all and must make decisions in life in order to avoid being perpetually mired in anxiety. In that moment, not because of my own strength or ability, but because of the belief that God was present with me on this journey, I chose to accept the college director position. In doing so I made the choice to participate in dealing with my anxieties as they came.

God was granting me this moment to be present with Him in this stage of my journey. I could not think about future steps, or future stages that the journey would require of me. I could only think about today. And in that moment I felt like God was saying to me, "Just take the job and trust Me with the rest." I distinctly remember answering God by saying, "I will take this job because I believe it's what You want for me and I love working with college students—but You are going to have to provide then. You are going to have to give me the ability to speak in front of others. I can't do this on my own."

Even today as I write I can clearly remember that conversation with God. That conversation has become the experience by which I try to counter the anxiety I feel when making decisions. Essentially I was saying to God, "I will do this. I will face my anxiety, but You are going to have to help me do this!"

If we are used to ignoring our anxieties and avoiding risks it can be quite hard and seem almost impossible for us to get to the place where we go to battle with them and prevail. We may be so used to losing that mental, emotional, and spiritual battle that we can't reimagine life any other way. Perhaps we have become stuck in our rut and held captive in our own lives as we have given the unseen force of anxiety free rein to run rampant within us. If so, we are granting anxiety permission to keep us from living the freedom of the life God has called us toward.

Like the disciples who had to reimagine life out of death and what a crucified Christ meant in their lives, we too must begin to do the hard work of reimagining what God wants to do with our anxiety. In a letter to his best friend, Eberhard Bethge, Dietrich Bonhoeffer captures this anxiety beautifully:

> I have long been fond of the time between Easter and Ascension. After all, here, too, there is great tension. How are human beings to endure earthly tensions if they know nothing of the tension between heaven and earth.[4]

A young adult woman came to see me one afternoon after anxiety had culminated in her life in such a way that she was beginning to do physical harm to herself. She was wondering more and more about whether suicide was an option for her. She was a college graduate in her early twenties. She was very smart and she constantly wondered what I was thinking in the therapy session, analyzing how I sat and what I said, and then interpreting what I must have thought about her.

She was one of those people who I love working with in the context of therapy. She had the courage to face her anxiety head-on. That's one of the reasons she came to therapy. One of the unfortunate misconceptions about therapy is that people think that they have to be "messed up" to go see a therapist. That idea is only encouraged by a Christian culture at large that often views going to therapy, like anxiety, as a sign of "weakness" or of "spiritual lethargy" in one's Christian faith. I think that is a travesty.

Every day I am witness to the miraculous courage of those who sit across from me and face themselves as they go to battle with their anxiety. It is these people who have courage and show strength. The psychiatrist Irvin Yalom commented on anxiety, saying, "Anxiety is a signal that one perceives some threat to one's continued existence."[5]

But you have the choice to decide what to do with that existential threat to your identity.

And so as we faced her anxiety together, I began the process of trying to help her reimagine what the purpose of the anxiety in her life was. She had always just assumed that anxiety was a malign force and that as a Christian it was something that needed to be destroyed and buried once and for all. She had been told by Christian friends, pastors, and people in the church community that if she could just get rid of her anxiety then she would be "right" with God. And when she was "right" with God, then she would know what to do with her life. Life would be good then.

But I said to her, "What if God put that anxiety in your life for a purpose? What if it is His way of guiding you? Maybe anxiety is like the warning lights on the dashboard of our car that tells us when something is going on inside of us? Those lights say, 'Pay attention to me.' So what if God has put anxiety in your life as a way for Him to say, 'Hey, pay attention to Me. I am trying to keep you from getting stuck and buried in your fears. Follow Me.' What if anxiety is God's catalyst to help you grow, because when you have the courage to face it you are right where God wants you? Maybe anxiety is God's way to make us uncomfortable so that we just don't continue being content with where we are, always in search of what is most comfortable for us?"

As the words rolled off my lips and into the audible space between us I could see from her curious and hesitant expression that this was a new thought for her. And it was definitely a foreign thought for her in the Christian culture in which she was raised and was currently participating.

But she wanted to believe this could be true. If that were true, then maybe God wasn't upset with her. Then maybe something wasn't wrong with her faith. Then maybe God was there in her midst about to do an amazing work.

This is something that I personally understood in the context of my own life. Eight years earlier when I was swiveling in that chair in that intern's office at Bel Air Presbyterian

Church, I was asking myself the same question. "God, I have lots and lots of anxiety right now as I'm thinking about whether or not to take this job. But are You wanting me to face my anxiety and take this job? Are You wanting me to enter into my anxiety so that I can grow as a person?"

In that moment I felt like a decision to not take the job was a choice to run from my fears. And that choice wouldn't just impact that moment and decision, but would begin to lay the groundwork for a pattern of avoiding my fears and seeking safety whenever anxiety arose. I was twenty-seven at the time but I pictured myself in my forties and saw someone who avoided anxiety and wasn't living the life God was beckoning me to bravely follow Him into. It reminds me of the scene in the movie *Gladiator* where Maximus, played by Russell Crowe, says to the cohort of soldiers before heading out into battle, "Brothers, what we do in life echoes in eternity."[6] How we choose to look at and handle anxiety today echoes into our future as well.

If God had meant for me to not be anxious, then He would have called me to some other vocation that didn't require weekly preaching, an activity that was a constant reminder of my ongoing struggle with stuttering.

What if, instead, God wanted me to be anxious? What if He was wanting me to lean into Him and be dependent upon His strength, rather than my weakness? Rather than running away from it or just trying to bury it, what if He wanted me to enter directly into that anxiety so that He could help me grow in ways that I could not even reimagine?

This is the pivotal question that we must wrestle with

because this is the crucial moment where anxiety shifts in its meaning for us and we begin to reimagine it in ways that are beneficial for our lives rather than destructive.

Does God want you to face your anxiety so that He can help you grow?

Are you sitting in your room at home poring over college applications, anxiously wondering what college to choose, fearful of making the wrong decision?

Are you lying in your bed at night filled with stress, debating about whether or not you chose the right career?

Are you sitting next to your spouse on the couch, blankly watching TV, but inside you are filled with dread because your marriage is on the rocks and you don't know what to do?

This is anxiety in your midst and God wants you to pay attention to it. He wants you to listen to it. For in your anxiety God is speaking to you and He is encouraging you to not stay content with where you are. In that anxiety God is calling you forth out of that false place of safety and into a stage-by-stage journey where He wants to help you grow with the aid of the anxiety that He has placed within you.

What I am saying about anxiety may seem like a paradox to you. It can have both good and bad outcomes. That is okay. That is its beauty.

The New Testament word *merimnao*[7] is the paradoxical word that the apostle Paul uses in the text of Philippians 4:6 where he encourages the church at Philippi, "do not be anxious about anything." The word, depending on context, carries the double meaning of "to be anxious" as well as "to care for." Paul certainly isn't saying that we should live without a care in the world, but rather that we are not to be "unduly concerned" about something. To care for something in a healthy way leads to positive action, while becoming unduly concerned leads to anxiety and worry.

There are things in life that we are to have healthy anxiety about because it is part of our inborn human condition. God designed us that way. When we pay attention to our anxiety we are operating in a healthy way. When we suppress that natural anxiety we open the door for anxiety to move from being something we are "to be concerned about" into unhealthy ways of functioning, and in directions where we are "unduly concerned." Psychiatrist and author Rollo May, commenting on Kierkegaard, has this to say about the difference between a neurotic and healthy state of anxiety:

> The healthy individual moves ahead despite the conflict, actualizing his freedom, whereas the unhealthy person retrenches to a "shut-in condition" sacrificing his freedom.[8]

For Kierkegaard, anxiety always increases with the more possibilities we have. Who hasn't experienced that anxiety when faced with a multitude of choices to make? As we move into anxiety it is healthy to be anxious about the unknowns, to have doubts, and to experience the struggle of life's transitions. This is a normal, healthy anxiety. It is when we don't deal with that normal, healthy anxiety and choose to avoid or bury it that it begins to do something insidious in our lives.

We find ourselves stuck and we develop the inability to even start something, let alone follow through. For Kierkegaard,

The Anxious Christian

healthy anxiety tells us, "I can." In that belief of "I can" you have the choice to say, "I did it," which is a normal, healthy anxiety. The other option is to say, "I can't" or "I won't," which is a sign that we have fallen to a neurotic, unhealthy anxiety.[9]

It is okay to be anxious, but don't hide and bury those anxieties in hopes that they may somehow get better or completely disappear. They won't. Instead, choose to face them and allow God to grow you in the process. It is an act of courage that you will not regret.

It wasn't until I was twenty-four years old that I first began to really wrestle with the idea that anxiety was perhaps a feeling that God had placed in my life to help bring about change. I had just finished reading Kierkegaard's seminal work *Fear and Trembling* and knew that I could never go back to thinking the same thoughts about my anxiety.

Kierkegaard's words were life-giving, resonating deeply with my own experience, letting me know that I was not alone in my anxiety and that I was not a bad Christian because I felt those things. All of a sudden I began to feel hope and his story of Abraham and Isaac became like a close friend as I began to really work through my own anxiety in a Christian culture that told me I was better off just moving past it as quickly as possible. Kierkegaard comments on God's testing of Abraham through the sacrificing of his son Isaac in Genesis 22 by saying,

> The ethical expression for what Abraham did is that he meant to murder Isaac; the religious expression is that he meant to sacrifice Isaac—but precisely in this contradiction

is the anxiety that can make a person sleepless, and yet without this anxiety Abraham is not who he is.[10]

It is in this paradox of not being anxious and yet being in a state of fear and trembling that God wants us (cf. Philippians 2:12). It is precisely in that in-between space that God calls us to listen and to act. It's in our fear and dread, in our worry and stress, and in our restlessness and sleepless nights that God is doing the work of transforming our lives and beckoning us to not stay as we are.

Discussion Questions

1. How much or how little has the death and resurrection of Christ informed who you are and how you live?

2. Have you ever tried to reimagine something negative that has happened in your life? What was it, and what was the outcome?

3. What is one anxiety you have today that you would like to begin the process of reimagining?

Exercise

Make a list of several anxieties that you are currently facing. As you look at each one, brainstorm and write down possible ways God might be using that anxiety to speak to you/to compel you to action. No option or idea is off-limits. Let this be a free-flowing exercise.

Prayer

God, I pray that You take my anxiety and that as I coura-geously face it by Your grace, You will use it in a power-ful way to shape me into the person You want me to become.

chapter five

Wrestling with God

"Taking a new step, uttering a new word, is what they fear most."[1]

FYODOR DOSTOEVSKY

I knew logically that God had not abandoned me in those times of feeling alone as I grew up. But my heart was not logical.

I could not escape the constant feeling that though I knew God was present in my life, it still felt like He had abandoned me. It was one thing to intellectually know something, but to really believe it with all my heart, soul, mind, and strength so that it was present in my behavior would take a lot of work.

About once a quarter, I have the privilege of being a staff therapist for The Hideaway Marriage Experience[2] in Amarillo, Texas. Through that experience I'm continually inspired by the courage couples have to face their greatest fears in their marriage. Watching them become aware of their pattern of feelings and behavior as they share their lives with the therapists and other couples in the room helps bring awareness to my own negative cycle (pain cycle)[3] of coping.

The approach we use at the retreat center is based on a model developed by Terry Hargrave and Shawn Stoever, and that can be found in the book *5 Days to a New Marriage*.[4] In the book, they talk about a therapeutic process for couple's work where they help couples become aware of and understand their negative pattern of interaction known as the *pain cycle*.[5] By doing this, couples can then begin to make positive changes in their marriage by developing healthy patterns of interaction with the *peace cycle*.[6] Unlike a lot of couples' marital work where change is dependent upon one's partner, the peace cycle promotes positive change in our own individual lives that is dependent upon God and the Truth that He says about us, rather than our partner. While I have spent most of my life trying to have someone else fill the void left by my negative emotions, through this method I was offered a new way. The solution was within myself, and founded in who God says I am.

But how does one get to the Truth when anxiety keeps them from even having the courage to face their fears or try something different?

It is a lifelong process that you can begin today, but it takes courage to face your anxiety and seek after God in such a way that a new way of coping behavior can be created.

Listening to God and Anxiety

It is very difficult to form new behaviors after we have spent most of our life mastering ones that we have instinctually performed time and time again. Terry Hargrave and

Franz Pfitzer in their book *Restoration Therapy* put it well when they make the observation:

> Somehow, even though we know that certain thoughts and behaviors are bad for us and are rooted in our own self-reactivity [negative patterns of coping], we return to those behaviors and usually find that these actions further assault our identities as human beings and our sense of closeness and safety in relationships. Old ideas die hard.[7]

Old ideas do die hard. It reminds me of the time that my wife and I began the process of trying to encourage our daughter, who was four at the time, to get rid of her security blankets. My daughter would carry around these blankets everywhere she went. Whether she was hurt, scared, tired, or in a happy mood, she would take the blanket and slowly stuff it into her mouth bit by bit by bit. It was a remarkable sight as my wife and I wondered if she were going to swallow the entire thing. But that's what brought her comfort and helped soothe any anxiety that she was feeling.

It's quite normal for children to have instinctual rituals that they can cling to in order to help them soothe their anxiety. But as adults it's not always as simple. We need to learn how to face our anxieties so that we can form new patterns of soothing ourselves and coping in healthy ways. When we stay in our rut, staying put when we are feeling familiar or comfortable, we remove ourselves from some of the greatest opportunities for growth.

It's hard to think of a single story in the Bible where God

comes to someone who is living a routine life and lets them just stay where they are. Instead, we more typically see God flip their life upside down, so that in the process they can reimagine a new way to live.

What if anxiety is your cue to begin this process of changing your life? What if anxiety is what gives you the signal that God is at work and that it is time to surrender yourselves to Him?

If you ignore the anxiety in your life you are ignoring your greatest opportunity for growth and change that is made available to you. To ignore your anxiety is to stay stuck in your old patterns and to live out the same old life that keeps you in a perpetual state of unhealthy and neurotic anxiety.

God does not want this for you. He does not want you to stay stuck. He does not want you to live the same old life day in and day out, performing the same negative patterns that keep you from drawing closer to Him. In fact, the apostle Paul in Ephesians 4:22–24 encourages us:

> in reference to your former manner of life . . . lay aside the old self, which is being corrupted in accordance with the lusts of deceit, and . . . be renewed in the spirit of your mind, and put on the new self, which in the likeness of God has been created in righteousness and holiness of the truth. (NASB)

I think that most of us would look at this passage and say, "I want to take off the old self and put on the new self." But we lose our courage when we realize that the process is more difficult than we had imagined. When we begin to battle the resistance that seeks to keep us stuck in our old ways of living, we lose heart and choose to follow the path of least resistance, aiming for that old, worn-out trail rather than venturing off the path and into something new.

If that is you, don't lose heart. You are not alone.

There are many of us living life that way. If you are full of anxiety and fearful of trying something new, God is walking alongside of you and He wants to help you envision a new life that is totally transformed through and through. He desires to see you grow and evolve into the person He is encouraging you to be, but you have to want to change.

Engaging Anxiety and God

One of my favorite Bible stories as a child was the story of Jacob wrestling with God. There was something very honest and authentic about that story. It had this sense of earthiness about it that I could connect with. That is, the story in the text just really came alive for me and was something I could wrap my hands around. Perhaps it was because I could identify with the wrestling. My brother, Wyatt, is two and a half years younger than me and I think that hardly a moment passed by in our childhood years when we weren't engaged in some type of wrestling duel. Even now we often gesture at one another as if we are about to engage in a rematch, but it's all for show as we quickly realize that our bodies are not as young and durable as they used to be.

There is something powerful in wrestling. As a boy, wrestling was the ultimate sign of strength as two people went one-on-one. As you wait for the other person to engage you, there is this overwhelming feeling of anxiety, knowing that once it begins you could be overtaken at any moment.

In May of 2011 I was sitting in a Catalyst Dallas learning lab where blogger and author Jon Acuff was the speaker. In that session Jon talked about the intimacy in wrestling. For in order to wrestle with someone you have to be up close to engage them in it. You can't wrestle with someone from a distance, but must be close, skin-on-skin, as every detail of that other person emerges in the intimate struggle.

The story of Jacob wrestling with God is not only a portrayal of a loving relationship played out in the act of a close, intense struggle, but was also the catalyst, spurred on by Jacob's anxiety, that ultimately led to Him being shaped in a new way.

We find Jacob in "great fear and distress" according to the text (Genesis 32:6–7). Anxiety had gotten the better of him. Jacob was at a crucial turning point in his life as he made preparations for his fight or flight, which is a natural reaction to one's anxiety. He was told that his brother was coming to meet him with four hundred men, so Jacob divided his people into two groups so that one group could flee if the other came under attack.

All the anxiety that Jacob felt upon hearing that his brother was approaching him with four hundred men must have been an overwhelming experience. But it was in that place, in all his anxiety, that God came to him. It was in Jacob's anxiety that God showed up and turned Jacob's life around and moved him in a new direction.

This is a story that I can identify with.

How many times have I felt like life was overwhelming and that large forces beyond my control were headed in my direction?

I imagine that as Jacob went to bed that night, lying alone in the camp, anxiety was knocking on his door. How could it not? This is such a beautiful text:

So Jacob was left alone, and a man wrestled with him till daybreak. When the man saw that he could not overpower him, he touched the socket of Jacob's hip so that his hip was wrenched as he wrestled with the man. Then the man said, "Let me go, for it is daybreak."

But Jacob replied, "I will not let you go unless you bless me."

The man asked him, "What is your name?"

"Jacob," he answered.

Then the man said, "Your name will no longer be Jacob, but Israel, because you have struggled with God and with humans and have overcome."

Jacob said, "Please tell me your name."

But he replied, "Why do you ask my name?" Then he blessed him there.

So Jacob called the place Peniel, saying, "It is because I saw God face to face, and yet my life was spared."

The sun rose above him as he passed Peniel, and he was limping because of his hip. Therefore to this day the Israelites do not eat the tendon attached to the socket of the hip, because the socket of Jacob's hip was touched near the tendon.

There are so many powerful things happening in this text (Genesis 32:24–32) that can give us insight into our own journey of facing anxiety.

Holding On, Letting Go, and Walking Away

In many circumstances, as we experience anxiety, we may be tempted not to face it. We may be tempted to turn the other way and not acknowledge that it is there. But if God uses anxiety in our lives as a way to help us grow, then we must not turn away from it. Instead, we must engage our anxiety in a grueling match as we wrestle with what it may mean for us in our lives. Like Jacob we must be willing to say, "I will not let go unless You bless me" (Genesis 32:26). Or, "God, I'm not going to let go of You until You help me use my anxiety for good in my life!"

The paradox is that in our very act of hanging on to God we are free to let go of our own lives and our anxiety, allowing God to take our anxiety and shape us in a powerful new way.

Anxiety keeps us in pursuit of God. We are too tempted to not seek after God when we think we have life figured out. But anxiety is God's way of encouraging us to not rest confidently in our own selves. Without anxiety we are too tempted to try to be comfortable, opting to choose the path of least resistance. But if we are going to follow God, then anxiety is one of our greatest allies to help spur us on if we are willing to listen to it and engage with it.

As Christians we want to be able to grasp God. We try so hard to gain control over God in a variety of ways. Maybe we try to control God through our theology and doctrine. Maybe we try to control God by listening to our own will over His will for our life. But God cannot be controlled. Jacob tried to control God by asking His name, surmising that if he could just know His name then God could be reduced to something identifiable, something controllable. But God cannot be reduced to an idea or to a name, but forever remains just out of our controlling grasp. As the theologian Karl Barth points out, "God is personal, but personal in an incomprehensible way, in so far as the conception of his personality surpasses all our views of personality."[8] Without anxiety we would be tempted to pull off to the side of the road and just stay put. Anxiety compels us toward God, but we can never fully grasp Him.

Wrestling is an act of intimately relating to another human being. Because you are up close, engaging all of the senses, there is a powerful exchange that happens between the two people wrestling. In that intimacy you learn things about that other person. They may be spoken or unspoken, but you get a sense of who that person really is. Wrestling with God and our anxiety is a transforming process—you engage in the struggle, and when you finally disengage, you are different. God has left a mark on you. Because of the battle, parts of your character are refined and shaped in a new way. No one leaves a wrestling match unchanged. The biblical scholar Phylis Trible comments:

In combat we wonder about the names of the demons. Our own names, however, we all too frightfully recognize. But yet we hold on, seeking a blessing: the healing of wounds and the restoration of health. If the blessing comes—and we dare not claim assurance—it does not come on our terms. Indeed, as we leave the land of terror, we limp.[9]

When Jacob finished wrestling with God he walked away a limping man. His match with God left not only a spiritual and emotional mark on who he was, but it defined him in a physical way as well. When we engage our anxiety, we engage God, and in that process we are transformed, marked by God in order that we may live life more abundantly and into the fullness that He desires for us.

Seeing God Face-to-Face

When we finally have the courage to face our anxiety and not let go, we are closer to finding out who we really are. As Jacob wrestled with God, clinging for his very life, God gave him a new name, saying, "Your name will no longer be Jacob, but Israel, because you have struggled with God and with humans and have overcome." I fear that most of us will never know who God really created us to be because we hide behind layers and layers of masks. When we hide behind our masks and are afraid to face our anxieties, we live a life less than what God has called us to. It's only when we face our anxieties that we enter into that intimate, relational wrestling match with God. And it's in that struggle that we gain a clearer sense of who we are as God speaks to us, even in the midst of our anxieties.

When you finally acknowledge your own anxiety and face it for what it is, then you enter into that reimagining process as God takes your anxiety and helps you follow Him into the places He is calling you toward. He is calling you into a relationship where your anxiety is dependent on Him and not the things you do. I love the insights of Henry Nouwen as he comments on Mark 1:9–11 where the gospel writer states,

> At that time Jesus came from Nazareth in Galilee and was baptized by John in the Jordan. Just as Jesus was coming up out of the water, he saw heaven being torn open and the Spirit descending on him like a dove. And a voice came from heaven: "You are my Son, whom I love; with you I am well pleased."

Nouwen astutely points out that in these verses we get a glimpse of Jesus before He has done any ministry that we know of. He has not healed the sick. He has not cast out demons. He is not the miracle worker that we see later on in the gospel. And yet, as He is preparing to enter into His ministry, His Father from heaven declares to Him, "You are my Son, whom I love; with you I am well pleased." Before Jesus has done anything that identifies Him with the Jesus we come to know in the gospels, His identity is secure in the relationship that He has with His Father. His Father loves Him because He is His son, not because He does bigger, better, and more things.

But Nouwen continues. Because of Jesus' identity resting firmly in the relationship He has with His Father, He is then able to go out into the wilderness where He is tempted by the devil to be relevant, powerful, and spectacular.[10] And though He is tempted, He doesn't need to perform and do things to be accepted for who He is. Rather, He can resist the temptation of having to constantly do more because He is His Father's son.

And it is then, and only then, that Jesus is able to go out and do the ministry that He was called to do.

Jacob had been praying to find favor in Esau's eyes in the midst of his anxiety (Genesis 32:5). He was fearful and worried about seeing his brother Esau again. In what I think is a most extraordinary scene, the favor that Jacob finds in Esau's eyes begins in his confrontation with God. It is in that very intimate relational act of wrestling with God that Jacob declares in the text "I saw God face to face" (Genesis 32:30).

In choosing to face his anxiety Jacob engaged God in an ultimate struggle for his identity and in the process not only saw God face-to-face, but was given a new name.

This is not the end of Jacob's anxiety though, but it is the turning point by which God gives him the grace to reimagine his anxiety in a new and productive way. Because Jacob was willing to grapple with anxiety and God, this then became the catalyst for the transformational encounter between he and his brother, Esau. Jacob moves from seeking to find favor in the eyes of God to finding favor in Esau's eyes, who he considers lord over him. But it was his encounter with God in the very act of facing and reimagining his anxiety that spurs him to likewise encounter Esau. So we find him declaring when he meets Esau that "to see your face is like seeing the face of God" (Genesis 33:10).

Terry Hargrave and Franz Pfitzer in their book *Restoration Therapy* talk about the importance of a person "finding and identifying the Truth about self."[11] If a person is going to be able to, in a sense, rewire their negative pattern of interaction between their feelings and coping behaviors that they have developed over a long period of time, there must be a Truth that they can cling to. They state,

> It is so natural for the individual that the assumptions that he or she makes about identity and safety are treated as truth for that individual. Unless this truth about identity or safety is challenged effectively, the individual often remains trapped in the primary feelings associated with lack of love and trustworthiness.[12]

In order for someone to be able to identify and anchor their life around a new truth, Hargrave and Pfitzer recommend the importance of self, others, and spiritual resources as aiding in that process.

The story of Jacob wrestling with God is a story about his encounter to identify the truth about who he was, in order that he could go out and live life differently. In order that he may live life in a transformed way as he pursued what God was calling him to be and to do. It's a story of Jacob's encounter with himself, with others, and with God.

When you and I have the courage to face our anxiety we

find ourselves immersed in the very intimate act of wrestling and struggling with God over what He is encouraging us to do with our lives. It is an opportunity for us to confront our fears and to see God face-to-face. We cannot control or manipulate God, but we can choose to engage Him in the midst of our anxieties. It is in this encounter with God that we are transformed. It is here that we are given a new name and a new identity that propels us in the direction that God is spurring us. We may walk away with a limp, but at least we had the courage to face our anxieties and to seek God in a way that many people never have the courage to do.

Shaped by Anxiety and God

My grandmother passed away at the age of ninety-three in September of 2009. She was one of the strongest and wisest people that I knew. She was born in 1916 and had lived through the Depression, multiple world wars, and a number of personal tragedies. But it was these struggles that really shaped who she was. When my mom died in 1986 my grandmother helped pick up the pieces and became a second mom to my brother and me. She was more alive and had more strength than most people I knew half her age.

One of the things that I really enjoyed about my grandmother was the way she told stories. She grew up on a farm and spent most of her life there, eventually selling it in 1995. Her stories were rich with metaphor and earthiness that was connected to everyday life and reality. And it was her farm and the way that she observed life that enriched her stories.

But in her life and in all the stories that she told you could sense a deep connection with God and His Word. I remember her always having this large well-read, underlined Bible next to her reading chair. Her Bible was always there, like a piece of furniture that never moved. But the text didn't remain there lifeless. It was this powerful, dynamic force that shaped her entire life. She immersed herself in God's Word every day and it came out in the way that she talked and served and loved. She did not have an easy life, but I remember her as one who always had the courage to face her anxieties and to wrestle with God in the daily struggles that she encountered.

I remember her telling me a story once that I think may have been the source of her strength to live such a God-filled, remarkable life. I was sitting with her on her couch when she turned to me and tears started to well up in her eyes. She said, "I was reading the story of the potter and the clay this morning. And do you know that when a potter is working with the clay he never takes his hands off the clay as he is shaping it." I replied, "Nana, I didn't know that. I've seen potters work with clay before, but I've never really thought about that." Then she looked into my eyes as we sat there face-to-face and she said as tears began to flow down her face, "And do you know the good Lord never takes His hand off of us?"

That was the shortest story she ever told me. More of an anecdotal remark on an observation she had made. But it is a story that has greatly influenced me and is a powerful reminder of what happens between God and us when we are engaged with Him in the struggle of our lives.

I love the text that my grandmother was referring to in Jeremiah 18:1–6:

> This is the word that came to Jeremiah from the Lord: "Go down to the potter's house, and there I will give you my message." So I went down to the potter's house, and I saw him working at the wheel. But the pot he was shaping from the clay was marred in his hands; so the potter formed it into another pot, shaping it as seemed best to him.
>
> Then the word of the Lord came to me: "O house of Israel, can I not do with you as this potter does?" declares the Lord. "Like clay in the hand of the potter, so are you in my hand, O house of Israel."

Jeremiah was instructed by the Lord to "go down to the potter's house," and as he arrives he sees the potter working on his wheel. The potter is sitting at his wheel with the clay in his hands, in the continual act of shaping it "as seemed best to him." Whatever fears and anxieties we have, whatever things we think mar us, the good news is that God has His hand on us. We are His clay and He is in the ongoing process of shaping and reshaping you into the person that He desires you to be.

For a long time I was fearful of relinquishing the illusion of control in my life. If I was not in control, hands on the wheel, then everything would just fall apart. But what the story of the potter and the clay continues to remind me of is that when I let go of things I am giving them to God. I'm allowing God to shape me into the person He wants me to become, rather than fighting Him for control of my life.

Every time I sit with my daughter and play with her Play Doh, I am reminded that God always has His hand on me, shaping and reshaping me. It is a struggle sometimes to get clay, or Play Doh, to take the shape that we want it to take. But eventually the clay yields to our hands as it begins to soften under our continual working and kneading of it. So too, in our anxiety when we yield to the hands of God, rather than hide and submerge it, we are allowing God to shape us.

It is possible that you have been living the same life, day in and day out, for way too long. God does not want you to just buckle down and live life in a cowering position. But He desires for you to listen to the anxiety within you. And when you listen to that anxiety, God wants you to engage Him in an intimate and up-close relationship. For it is in that up-close relationship that the Great Potter can begin to do the strenuous work of reshaping and reforming the clay that is your life. It is then, and only then, that you enter into the transforming work of taking off the old self and putting on the new self.

It is not an easy thing for you to face your anxieties. Your anxieties have more than likely caused you much pain and many sleepless nights. Your anxieties have kept you in a steady state of limbo between decisions, and in constant worry about whether you are heading in the right direction.

But like the clay, God wants to take your anxieties and reimagine them. He wants to hold them in His hand and reshape them into something beautiful.

Discussion Questions

1. What are some of the "old ideas" (patterns of feelings/coping behaviors) that you have in your life that you are having a hard time addressing?

2. What would it look like for God to take those "old ideas" and transform them into something new and life-giving for you?

Exercise

1. Sometimes we need to do something with our hands to help us also engage our minds and hearts. Take a piece of clay or Play Doh and play with it, shaping it into whatever shape or image you desire. As you do this, reflect on the work of God in your life. Do you allow Him to shape you like clay?

2. What would you need to do to submit to Him, allowing Him to shape you?

Prayer

God, I ask that You give me the courage to engage You, and that as I do that, I hold on to You and let go of anxiety, allowing You to shape that anxiety into a beautiful thing in my life in order that I may be transformed more in Your image and into who You are desiring for me to be.

chapter six

Getting Intentional

"Slay that dragon once,
and he will never have power over you again."[1]

STEVEN PRESSFIELD, *Do the Work*

I f we choose to live our lives long enough without a sense of intention, the anxiety that we feared to face from the outset can grow into a monster too overwhelming to face at all. There's a story of a young boy named Billy Bixbee who wakes up one morning, surprised to find a small dragon in his room "about the size of a kitten." As the day continues Billy tries drawing attention to the dragon and his ever-increasing size, only to hear his mother retort, "There's no such thing as a dragon!" Eventually the dragon in their midst becomes so large that he becomes hard not to notice. The story ends with the dragon shrinking back down to his kitten size, whereupon there is this exchange: "I don't mind dragons THIS size," said Mother. "Why did it have to grow so BIG?" "I'm not sure," said Billy, "but I think it just wanted to be noticed."[2]

That book was given to me by my friend Keenan Barber who is the young adult pastor at Bel Air Presbyterian Church in Los Angeles. He gave it to me one weekend after he unwittingly played a role in helping me face my own dragon of anxiety. I will come back to the duel with my dragon later in the book, but it reminds me of the words of writer Steven Pressfield in his book *Do the Work*, which along with his book *The War of Art* were crucial in helping me face my anxiety as I wrote this book. Pressfield states,

> Here's one thing I can tell you and you can take this to the bank:
> Slay that dragon once, and he will never have power over you again.
> Yeah, he'll still be there. Yeah, you'll still have to duel him every morning. And yeah, he'll still fight just as hard and use just as many nasty tricks as he ever did. But you will have beaten him once, and you'll know you can beat him again. That's a game changer.
> That will transform your life.[3]

When we are more intentional in our lives, we better position ourselves to allow God to use our anxiety for good. And in doing so, we must face that dragon of anxiety that has taken up residence within us.

In October of 2008 my wife and I finally chose to face the growing dragon in our midst. We decided to choose to not let life's circumstances and our bad choices keep us enslaved to a life that we didn't want, and didn't believe God wanted for us either. After two graduate degrees, a sunken house market in Los Angeles, and frivolous credit card spending, we found ourselves $115,000 in debt.

We were discouraged and overwhelmed.

We were "sick and tired of being sick and tired" of all the debt. I had heard that phrase from Dave Ramsey who I discovered on the radio in our move to Dallas. I had known of Dave before, but I just thought he was that unrealistic-sounding guy who told people to cut up their credit cards and pay cash for everything. But the more I listened to him, the more I was drawn in. He was intentional, and that stuck out in a culture that is very unintentional.

I still remember my wife and me purchasing his book *The Total Money Makeover* and audio CDs. For a couple of nights we sat down and listened through the audio CDs and we worked through the workbook. We were stunned. Could it really be this easy to get out of debt? No tricks? Just straight-forward hard work?

We realized that this was just one area of our life that we had become passive about and wanted to become more intentional with.

Those nights of sitting down at the kitchen table with Heather while our baby daughter Hayden slept were the turning points for us. We made a promise then to just attack the debt with "gazelle intensity," as Dave talked about.

So for thirty-one months we drastically changed our lifestyle.

We moved from being passive to intentional in this one area of our life. And we discovered that when you choose to be intentional in one area of your life, that intentionality tends to bleed over into other areas of your life, creating positive change at multiple levels.

We stopped eating out, except for an occasional inexpensive meal every few weeks. We stopped buying clothes. We drastically cut entertainment. Probably went to fewer than ten movies in those thirty-one months. We cut magazine subscriptions. We didn't buy new gadgets or spend money on music. We stopped buying books and started visiting our local library. We stopped going to coffee shops and made our coffee at home. I stopped buying lunch at work and started packing my lunch. We drew names at Christmas while Heather and I limited our gifts to each other to $25, which really drew out our creativity. We only took one vacation, a free vacation that unfortunately was paid for using the points we had racked up on our credit card debt. We were learning as we went. And we continued to drive nine- and twelve-year-old cars with 136,000-plus miles on both of them.

Looking back we think we could have knocked off that debt even sooner, but life got crazy along the way and emergencies happened and we lost motivation and will at times. One of the most crucial turning points for us was when we saw Dave Ramsey speak live at the Potter's House in Dallas in March of 2010.

Seeing Ramsey speak live was just the kick in the pants we needed. I think it was the message of being more intentional that renewed our focus and purpose. You see, we had paid off $60,000 between July 2008 and March of 2010, so we felt pretty good about ourselves. Our friends couldn't believe how much we paid off. But after seeing Dave live we realized we had to pick up the intensity or it would drag on for us. So from March of 2010 to May 19, 2011, we paid off $55,000.

As we sent off that final debt payment on May 19, 2011, we looked at each other and almost couldn't believe it. For our entire marriage we had always had some kind of debt hanging around our necks like a slowly tightening noose. And now we finally felt free. Because we chose to become intentional about becoming debt free, our decisions aren't held captive by finances, and we feel the freedom to make choices we wouldn't have been able to make years ago.

We had always believed before that somehow we would be rescued. Rescued by some new job, some huge bonus, or perhaps winning the lottery, even though we didn't play.

But waiting around to be rescued by someone or something got us nowhere and left us feeling powerless. We realized we had to take responsibility for our debt and radically eliminate it.

We had to be intentional.

This is anxiety at work in a practical day-to-day sense. It was our continued anxiety about our debt that eventually stirred us to action. Because we listened to our anxiety, our anxiety became the catalyst for change and growth in our lives. Our anxiety gave us the clarity we needed to be focused and intentional.

As a licensed marriage and family therapist I tell couples that their marriages only improve when they each take responsibility for themselves, and stop waiting for, or pointing at their partner, to change. Only when we own our issues and take responsibility for ourselves will true change happen in a marriage. And this is not true just in our marriages but in our lives overall. Only when we stop blaming others and take responsibility for ourselves can we pursue change.

Radically Pursuing Change

On the first morning of The Hideaway Experience[4] when four couples and two therapists gather to begin four days of intensive marriage work, we begin with a challenge for couples to radically pursue change in their lives. I love how my friend and cotherapist Todd Sandel urges couples to realize that the issues they are now experiencing in their marriages are too painful for them to continue doing things the same way. You need to "radically pursue change" he tells the couples, if they want to actually see change in their lives and in their marriages. It's really a call for them to be intentional about themselves and in their marriages. It's a call for them to no longer be passive observers and to no longer play the role of victims in their relationship with one another.

Change doesn't occur in our lives and in our relationships without intention.

We have to want to change. We have to choose to change. We have to be intentional in bringing about the positive growth that we desire to see in our life.

Anxiety stirs us to action when we are careful to pay attention to it. But when we ignore our anxiety we tend to lie helpless like the "invalid" in the gospel story of John 5:1–9:[5]

Some time later, Jesus went up to Jerusalem for one of the Jewish festivals. Now there is in Jerusalem near the Sheep

Gate a pool, which in Aramaic is called Bethesda and which is surrounded by five covered colonnades. Here a great number of disabled people used to lie—the blind, the lame, the paralyzed. One who was there had been an invalid for thirty-eight years. When Jesus saw him lying there and learned that he had been in this condition for a long time, he asked him, "Do you want to get well?"

"Sir," the invalid replied, "I have no one to help me into the pool when the water is stirred. While I am trying to get in, someone else goes down ahead of me."

Then Jesus said to him, "Get up! Pick up your mat and walk." At once the man was cured; he picked up his mat and walked.

"Do you want your marriage to get well?" Todd asks the couples. It seems like an obvious if not funny question to ask of people who have made a huge investment to come to an intensive session in order to work on their marriages. But the reality is, many of them will ignore the anxiety that brought them to the retreat, while they continue to be passive observers and watch life go by without any intention. Just because they are there doesn't mean they are ready to be intentional in their lives or their marriages. Like the invalid sitting by the pool year after year, passively watching people enter into the pool and become healed, we too often sit on the sidelines watching everyone else make the changes we want in our lives.

So, do you want to change? Do you want to grow? Or are you going to continue to just stay where you are?

Fostering Intention in Our Lives

One of the drawbacks of a seminary and graduate school education is that it can tend to teach you how to overcomplicate things. Fortunately, pastoral ministry and counseling can be a good antidote to the complexity as the people you come across in those contexts are wanting you to just keep it simple and to the point. Jesus always seemed to have had a way to steer through the chaos and focus on the essentials while keeping it to the point in the process. I love the story in the gospels (Matthew 22:37; Mark 12:30; Luke 10:27) where Jesus is tested by the Pharisees as to what is the greatest commandment in the Law:

> On one occasion an expert in the law stood up to test Jesus. "Teacher," he asked, "what must I do to inherit eternal life?"
>
> "What is written in the Law?" he replied. "How do you read it?"
>
> He answered, "'Love the Lord your God with all your heart and with all your soul and with all your strength and with all your mind; and, 'Love your neighbor as yourself.'" (Luke 10:25–27)

Jesus, affirming the lawyer's answer, reduces all of the law down to a person loving God with their heart, soul, strength, and mind, and their neighbor as themselves. To love God in this way is a very intentional act on our part and I like how Jesus simplifies it for us by helping us focus on four specific areas of our lives. I know that life is messy and hard to categorize many times, but this response by Jesus provides healthy parameters for our lives that allow us to focus our intention with more specificity.

I believe that focusing on these areas can encourage us to foster intention in our lives in order that we may better face our anxiety and all the challenges it presents. Because when we choose to be intentional about specific areas of our lives it allows us to reduce levels of unhealthy anxiety that we may not be addressing. Being intentional gives us focus to look at anxiety and reimagine it in healthy ways in our lives.

Fostering Your Heart

From as early as I can remember, the heart was the symbol of love. It was the symbol that said I wanted to be in relationship with someone else. It signifies a relational connection and implies an engagement of emotions and feelings. Cambridge professor David Ford talks about the heart in this way:

"Heart" is a way of talking about that dimension of our self where memory, feeling, imagination, and thinking come together. The heart is like a home for all the concerns of our lives, where our identity is sorted out year after year. Above all it is inhabited by images of other people and of ourselves in relation to them. Our hearts are filled with the faces and voices of those before whom we live. These are the members of our "community of the heart."[6]

In order for us to live more intentional lives, one of the areas that we need to foster is our relational connection. We need to be intentional about how we foster our heart. When we foster this area of our lives, it is one of the ways that we demonstrate our love for God. God has designed us to be in relationship with one another as we see in the perfect model of the interrelational connection between Father, Son, and Spirit in the Trinity. If we are made in God's image (Genesis 1:27), then one of the ways that we love Him is demonstrated by the ways in which we love, relate, and stay connected to those around us.

Relational anxiety is a common occurrence in many relationships, hindering a deep emotional connection that so many people desire. We find ourselves in relationships, anxious about what others think of us and anxious about how we feel about ourselves in those relationships. So when we choose to be intentional in this area of our life we are choosing to face those relational anxieties that exist but that we often try to push below the surface.

Here are some simple suggestions for how you can foster your heart:

- Plan date nights with your spouse or significant other.
- Participate in a weekly Bible study, book club, or hobby group.
- Get together with friends on a regular basis for meals.
- Spend time getting to know your classmates or co-workers better.

Getting Intentional

Fostering Your Soul

The meaning of "soul" is hard to communicate, though we have ideas of what it means in our lives. Soul is that deep-seated psychological and spiritual connection that I have with God and with others. To love God with your soul is to love Him in ways that are hard to define, but there are ways of thinking about it that can help us more intentionally foster it in our lives. As author Thomas Moore points out:

> The soul makes you a unique person, a human being with deep feelings and the capacity for strong relationships. Your soul comes alive in cherished friendships, family gatherings, and the care you bring to your home. And yet, it isn't easy to define or even describe with clarity. It's the mystery element in your sense of who you are and in the world you engage with.[7]

I like to think of soul as the way that I foster a deep connection with God. When I love God with my soul, I am practicing things and living out ways that intentionally foster my spiritual life. Reading Scripture, praying, and worshiping are just some of the ways that I am intentional about fostering my soul and practicing my faith.

Anxiety is often found in this area of our lives, creating fear and doubt when unattended to. I believe one of the reasons that so many people struggle with their faith is that they choose to ignore the anxiety in the soul connection between themselves and God, and instead desperately try to put on a "game face" for others around them. So when we choose to be intentional in this area of our lives we are opening up more authentic means of relating to God, rather than attempting to appear spiritual to others.

Below are some simple suggestions for how you can foster your soul:

- Daily reading of God's Word
- Listening in silence
- Devotional reading
- Journaling
- Listening to encouraging music
- Worship

Fostering Your Strength

I have always loved to run. I loved racing other kids on the playground when I was in elementary school, and that love continued on through high school where I ran the 300-meter hurdles and the 4 x 400 relay. Running was something I just enjoyed doing, but after the required practice and discipline of high school sports, my running took on a more sporadic nature. In 2006, my brother suggested that we run the Chicago Marathon together. I thought he was crazy, but I agreed. In October 2006 I completed my first marathon in 4:13. I have been hooked ever since.

When I chose to be intentional about running a marathon, it required that I become intentional about training for the race. What I discovered along the way was that the physical training and pushing myself led to a deeper spiritual connection and to more faithfully loving God. The quote from my favorite boyhood movie *Chariots of Fire* was now more than just a cool quote. Eric Liddell's belief became a living reality for me when he said, "I believe God made me for a purpose, but he also made me fast. And when I run I feel His pleasure."[8] Now I may not be fast, but when I run I do feel God's pleasure, and it is one of the healthy ways that I constructively use the anxiety in my life in order to grow spiritually. I love the way that Eugene Peterson was intentional about his running, and through that fostered a connection between the act of running and his relationship with God:

> I began having fun, enjoying again the smooth rhythms of long-distance running, the quietness, the solitude, the heightened senses, the muscular freedom, the texture of the ground under my feet, the robust embracing immediacy of the weather—wind, sun, rain, snow . . . whatever. Soon I was competing in 10K races every month or so, and then a marathon once a year. Running developed from a physical act to a ritual that gathered meditation, reflection, and prayer into the running.[9]

Exercise is one of the helpful ways that people cope with and reduce unhealthy levels of anxiety in their lives. But I also believe exercise is one of the ways that helps you reimagine anxiety in a positive light that encourages you to grow from it, rather than just seeking to bury and eliminate the anxiety where you then gain no benefit from it. When you are intentional about engaging in physical activity you are opening up one of the ways that you love God with all of your strength.

Here are some simple suggestions for how you can foster your strength:

- Go for daily walks/runs.
- Train for a race of any distance.
- Go to the gym (lift weights, swim, Pilates, etc.).
- Work in your garden or yard.
- Do housework.

Fostering Your Mind

Loving God with our minds is probably one of the areas most familiar to us living in a Western culture overly concerned with book and head knowledge. We often equate loving God to just studying and knowing the right answers. Despite our tendency to overemphasize this area, fostering our mind is a vital aspect of our spiritual lives. Theologian Carl Henry wrote, "Training the mind is an esential responsibility of the home, the church, and the school. Unless evangelicals prod young people to disciplined thinking, they waste—even undermine one of Christianity's most precious resources."[10]

When you engage in the activity of your mind, whether in school, work, or hobby, you are demonstrating one way that God has created you and in which you can lovingly respond to Him. God has created us with a remarkable capacity to think, but it is often our intellectual life that fosters a lot of anxiety.

The following are some simple suggestions for how you can foster your mind:

- Read a book.
- Take a class.
- Join a Bible study.
- Learn a new language.
- Listen to free sermons or lectures on the Internet.

Start with You

Something that I had always overlooked in Luke 10:27 was the last part of the verse where Jesus encourages his audience to "Love your neighbor as yourself." Jesus presupposes that in order for us to love others we must already love ourselves first. *What? Seriously? How have I missed that all these years?* We live in a culture that encourages us to always focus on the other person. That is not a bad quality in and of itself, but if in the process we are not focused on loving ourselves, or being intentional in our own lives, then we have nothing to offer those around us. We have nothing to give our neighbor if our own well from which we draw living water is empty and dry. Perhaps you focus on others so much as a way to deflect and ignore the things in your life that God wants you to be intentional about and grow from. *If Jesus felt the need to withdraw and pray, in order that He could minister out of an overflow of His own heart, soul, mind, and strength,*

then why do we feel like we are somehow exempt from that
(Luke 5:16)?

If you want to radically pursue change in your life then
stop waiting for everyone else around you to change first.
Stop waiting for someone's choices and decisions to alter
your life in the ways that you desire. Stop waiting for someone else to come along and bear your anxiety for you. If you
really want to change your life, then intentionally begin the
change in your own life first. Be intentional about fostering
your own heart, soul, mind, and strength. When you do that,
you will actually have something to offer your neighbor.

Fostering Thankfulness

After being introduced to the practice of Lent in 1999, I
could no longer approach Easter without being more intentional about the time leading up to Easter Sunday. I had
begun to realize that my lack of intention about the Lenten
season had been robbing me of the joy of Easter Sunday and
reducing my capacity to really participate in the full expression of what Christ's resurrection exemplifies for my life as a
Christian. So over the years I have tried various things during
Lent. I have given up things (e.g., fast food, sugar, carbona-
tion). And I have added things (e.g., prayer, retreats, devo-
tionals). I desired intention in my Lenten practices but they
still seemed to lack real clarity or purpose.

So in the spring of 2011, I proposed a new idea to my
wife, Heather, for our Lenten practices. "What if every day
we write down one thing we are thankful for on a piece of

paper? We can then take those pieces of paper and put them up on the wall as a sort of mosaic of our thankfulness this Lenten season." She loved the idea, and so Heather, daughter Hayden, and I began a new practice of daily telling each other what we were thankful for and keeping track of it on simple pieces of white printer paper.

About a week and a half into our new tradition, I really came to understand just how powerful being intentional in our family life was becoming. One evening my three-and-a-half-year-old daughter Hayden came up to me on her own and said, "Daddy, what are you thankful for today?" Our choice to become more intentional was shaping our family in a new way and it was helping us foster a new posture of gratitude in our family life.

Something that I began to realize during this process was that the anxieties that I was feeling in my life at the time were starting to disappear. They were starting to disappear because I was becoming more intentional in my life in several areas, and because our goal of fostering a life of thankfulness was helping us reimagine our anxiety in a new way. Instead of being anxious about the debt we were trying so hard to pay down, we were thankful about the jobs we had, the money we made, and the progress on the debt we were making. Instead of being anxious about the hours I still needed to officially become licensed as a marriage and family therapist in the state of Texas, I was thankful for what I had accomplished and the small number of hours I had left to complete. Instead of being anxious about writing this book and my daily struggle of thinking this rough draft was a complete failure, I was thankful for the opportunity to write and for the entire creative process.

Below are some suggestions for fostering thankfulness in our lives:

- Write down one thing every day you are thankful for. Post the notes on a wall to form a collage of your thankfulness.
- Verbally communicate with someone what you are thankful for each day. Expressing it verbally makes it even more real and vibrant.
- Use author Ann Voskamp's wonderful book *One Thousand Gifts: A Dare to Live Fully Right Where You Are*[11] as a helpful guide in this process.

Fostering Prayerfulness

I hate to admit this, but I have always had a hard time praying in the sense of a daily quiet time or devotional. There have been periods of my life when I have been able to do this for a season, while other seasons my prayer life seemed all but dried up. I've wondered at times if I have treated prayer as a very legalistic discipline rather than as a form of communication with God that requires the care and nurturing of a relationship, like other relationships around me. Prayer has been a source of anxiety to say the least.

It's a very different thing to think of prayer in the context of being intentional about fostering a relationship with the Creator of the universe, versus something that I have to do out of duty each day because I am a Christian. Over the years I have tried various things from devotions, to prayer in the morning, to prayer at bedtime, to just trying to talk with God throughout the day. Often I just listen and see what He may be saying to me. In the gospel of Matthew, Jesus gives His disciples a very intentional model for prayer. In Matthew 6:9–13, Jesus says:

> This, then, is how you should pray:
> "Our Father in heaven,
> hallowed be your name,
> your kingdom come,
> your will be done,
> on earth as it is in heaven.
> Give us today our daily bread.
> And forgive us our debts,
> as we also have forgiven our debtors.
> And lead us not into temptation,
> but deliver us from the evil one."

Without even commenting on the rich theology in this passage of Scripture, what is quite evident is that Jesus models a prayer that requires a sense of purposefulness in our lives. Embedded in the prayer are intentional acts of praise, thankfulness, forgiveness, and more. No matter how we choose to pray and communicate with God, one thing it does require of us is doing it with intention. When we foster a prayerful life, it is just one way that we maneuver ourselves to be in a position of reimagining our anxiety in a helpful way, and allowing God to speak to us through it.

Bonhoeffer reminds us that prayer and the cultivation of a relationship with God is not dependent upon our moods or a passive activity. It requires that we practice with a sense of willfulness:

> The person who waits upon moods is impoverished. If the painter only wanted to paint when in the mood for it, he would not get very far. In religion, as in art and science, along with the times of high excitement, there are times of sober work and practice. We must practice our communion with God, otherwise we will not find the right tone, the right word, the right language, when God surprises us with his presence.[12]

Here are a few suggestions for fostering prayerfulness in our lives:

- Find a text of Scripture that you can use to meditate on and share your thoughts with God. It's not necessary that you pray a certain prayer, but that you are intentionally reflecting upon God's Word and communicating with Him.
- Set aside ten minutes a day to sit in silence, listening to God. It's okay if you feel like you don't hear Him speaking to you. Foster this practice.
- Write out a short prayer each day (1–4 sentences.)

Discussion Questions

1. What is the biggest hindrance in your life to you living in a more intentional and purposeful way?

2. What is one thing that you have noticed in your life that requires more intention on your part? Why haven't you taken action yet?

3. What is one thing that you are thankful for today?

Exercises

1. Take out a piece of paper, drawing four columns across the page. Label each column for one of the four areas of our life that we can foster (i.e., heart, soul, strength, mind). Write down just one intentional practice for each category that you will commit to for the next three months.

2. After three months have passed, come back to this exercise and reevaluate how the intentional fostering of these four areas of your life helped you not only manage but reimagine your anxiety in a new way.

Prayer

In Psalm 56:3, King David states, "When I am [anxious], I put my trust in you." I like this intentional prayer in the psalm that helps us face our fears. I want to use this prayer as a way for us to look at our anxiety (I have substituted the word afraid *with* anxious*).*[13]

• Reflect on Psalm 56:3.

- Read Psalm 56:3 out loud over and over until it feels like it's a prayer of authenticity for you.

- Follow these three steps: (1) When I am anxious, I will acknowledge my feeling of anxiety. I will be emotionally honest, and not bury what I am feeling. (2) As I acknowledge my feelings of fear, I will also think right thoughts and remind myself of God's truth. (3) Then I will reset my will to do God's will; that is, I will acknowledge that anxiety has caused me to become paralyzed, but in thinking right thoughts, I will go ahead and do what God wants me to do.

- Repeat the Psalm 56:3 prayer a few times, putting it in your own words. It's not necessary that you come to a place today where you are one hundred percent confident you will do this. What is necessary is that you are intentional about moving toward allowing God to work on the anxiety in your life.

chapter seven

Creating Boundaries and Space

"Love consists in this, that two solitudes *protect and touch and greet each other."*[1]

RAINER MARIA RILKE

Letters to a Young Poet

The only way you will grow as a person and establish healthy boundaries in the process is by moving closer to your in-laws. Sure, it's easier to just keep the distance of states between you, but that won't help you in establishing healthy boundaries."

That was the suggestion of my therapist in session one day as I shared with him my anxiety of being newly married and trying to establish our "new family identity," while at the same time trying to figure out how to be a part of our larger family. Even though I have wonderful parents and in-laws, I found myself wrestling with my identity, fearful of losing myself as I merged into a new and larger family system. It was hard enough to figure out who I was in a new marriage with Heather, let alone trying to figure out who we were as a couple.

In order for me to manage my anxiety, it just felt easier to keep distance between the relationships where I was trying to figure out who I was. As long as my parents stayed in Scottsdale, Arizona, and Heather's parents stayed in Roanoke, Texas, then I felt like it would give me time to figure out who I was while living in Pasadena, California. It would give us time to figure out who Rhett and Heather Smith were. In that time I figured we could establish our identities and set in place some healthy boundaries. What my therapist helped me see was that I was actually avoiding the anxiety that would help me grow as a person as I was deflecting the responsibility of setting boundaries with people I was in relationship with. Though this process is full of all kinds of anxiety, it is the road for real relational growth and healthy interaction with others in our lives.

What I really wanted to do was avoid my anxiety and just keep the distance so I wouldn't have to actually work on establishing and maintaining healthy boundaries, which is a much more difficult task. It's easier to just cut people off or keep them at arm's length. It's much more difficult to establish our identity and healthy boundaries when we are in a face-to-face relationship with someone day in and day out, but that's where the real work begins. It doesn't begin by keeping people at a distance, where you control when to engage or not engage.

At some point in our journey, usually in early adulthood, we begin to wrestle with the idea of boundaries in our lives. We begin asking ourselves the question, "Where do I begin and end in relationship to you?" Because if we know where we begin and end in relationship with someone, then we can more clearly understand and define who we are as a person. It gives us a stronger sense of self and identity. And when we know who we are, and we exercise healthy boundaries, we are also better able to manage our own anxiety.

What Is a Boundary?

We hear people talk about boundaries a lot, but what really is a boundary, and what does it look like in our lives?

Well, there is a lot of literature on the topic of boundaries, but for our purposes, the definition that Henry Cloud and John Townsend provide in their classic book *Boundaries* is the most helpful. I like the way they define boundaries because I think they explain it in a simple way that makes sense for our lives. They state,

> Boundaries define us. They define what is me and what is not me. A boundary shows me where I end and someone else begins, leading me to a sense of ownership.
>
> Knowing what I am to own and take responsibility for gives me freedom. If I know where my yard begins and ends, I am free to do with it what I like. Taking responsibility for my life opens up many different options. However, if I do not "own" my life, my choices and options become very limited. . . .
>
> The Bible tells us clearly what our parameters are and how to protect them, but often our family, or other past relationships, confuses us about our parameters.
>
> In addition to showing us what we are responsible for,

boundaries help us to define what is not on our property and what we are not responsible for. We are not, for example, responsible for other people. Nowhere are we commanded to have "other-control," although we spend a lot of time and energy trying to get it![2]

I like the image of a boundary being like that of a property line around a yard. That image helps me better understand what defines a boundary and how I may apply it to my life. When I was between the ages of seven and ten I was obsessed with kicking soccer balls against the back of my house. I would do it all day long with about six or seven soccer balls that my brother, Wyatt, and I had. It didn't matter if he was playing goal keeper or I was out there by myself, I would kick the soccer balls against the wall over and over and over again. The problem with this though was that I would often kick one of the balls over the wall into our neighbor's yard, until eventually all of the soccer balls were over the fence.

When all of our soccer balls were over our fence and in our neighbor's yard, I figured that I had a couple of options. I could a) hop the neighbor's fence and get the soccer balls myself; or b) knock on my neighbor's door and ask them to retrieve the soccer balls for me. This became a dilemma for me since some days I could kick all of the soccer balls over the fence within an hour.

More often than not, I chose to jump over our fence, but I never knew what kind of reaction I would get from my neighbors when they saw me there in their backyard. Sometimes they would be okay with it because it saved them the hassle of having to get the soccer balls for me, and sometimes they would be upset because it felt like an intrusion on their privacy. On the occasions where I chose to walk next door and ring the doorbell, I would also get a mixed reaction. Sometimes they were happy to get the soccer balls for me, and other times they seemed pretty fed up with having to constantly go in their backyard and throw them back over.

Because our soccer balls kept ending up in our neighbor's yard, and because our fence was the boundary line between our two backyards, this back and forth exchange began to create a process by which our boundaries were being negotiated. Because I was always kicking the soccer balls over the fence, we eventually had to decide on some rules for how they would be retrieved. That is, we had to decide on some defined boundaries for when this happened. Though my neighbor and I had a defined boundary between our yards, it was the day-to-day talking and negotiating that helped us establish a healthy boundary between us, helping me better understand what I could and couldn't do when it came to the soccer balls going over the fence.

It may sound silly talking about soccer balls and fences when we think about boundaries, but I have found that this image has helped me as I establish boundaries in relationships with other people. In every relationship there is a boundary line. Sometimes it is visible, like the space between people as they talk, or the way that people decide to communicate (that is, in person, phone, text, email, etc.). Other times the boundary is invisible such as emotional or spiritual boundaries that we have agreed upon for ourselves, but that others may not know about—like when we avoid a particular person because of their negative influence on us.

But whether the boundary is invisible or visible, we know if someone has crossed our boundary. It feels like a violation when someone crosses the line, ignoring the boundary we have established between us. Sometimes a person chooses to intentionally cross a boundary that we have established such as deciding on a date to cross a physical boundary that had been previously agreed on. And other times people inadvertently cross our boundaries because they don't know the boundaries exist, such as when a person might call our home late at night, not knowing we don't take calls after a certain hour.

Boundary as Self-Care

Why are boundaries so important for us to establish? Because setting a boundary is the ultimate act of self-care in our lives. We set boundaries because we care about ourselves. Author Melody Beatie rightly points out that

> The goal of having and setting boundaries isn't to build thick walls around ourselves. The purpose is to gain enough security and sense of self to get close to others without the threat of losing ourselves, smothering them, trespassing, or being invaded. Boundaries are the key to loving relationships.[3]

In short, establishing healthy boundaries is just one way that we take care of ourselves as we interact in relationships with other people.

So if setting boundaries is how we take care of ourselves, then why are we so bad at it?

And why do Christians in particular have such a hard time setting healthy boundaries with other people?

I think it's because we live in a Christian culture that views self-care as an act of selfishness. That somehow when we pay any attention to ourselves, or take time to care for ourselves, we are ignoring the needs of others around us. We are taught that to care for others means not to place ourselves at all in the equation. To think of ourselves may elicit criticisms from others like, "You are self-absorbed, self-centered, not out-wardly focused, etc." We hope to avoid at all costs being called "selfish."

Jesus commanded us to "love your neighbor as yourself."

In order for us to love others we must love ourselves. In order for us to serve others we must love ourselves. It is out of this self-love that grace flows so that we can love those around us and continue to keep our eyes on those who are in need of the grace that God has given us to extend to others. But the extension of grace in others' lives begins with the living out of grace in our own lives.

Many Christians live unhealthy lives because they believe the lie that in order to adequately love others and put others before themselves they must exclude themselves in the process. This is most noticeable in the lack of healthy boundaries that many leaders have in their personal and work lives. Their lack of boundaries and therefore care of themselves (self-care) is glaringly absent. When we do not adequately care for ourselves and set healthy boundaries we cannot care for and give to others. It's not possible. Sure, maybe for a season, but not long term. Before long you will be burned out.

When we don't begin by looking at our own life and the work of God in it, we cannot venture out into the lives of others. If God sent His only Son to die for my sins, then He must have thought I was important enough. This love and grace of God is affirmed in my own life. Recognizing this, I can move out to those around me and let the overflow of that grace and love extend to others.

Sabbath Keeping and Creating Space

I speak quite frequently about the topic of "margin" in my work with families. *How do families create "white space" on the calendar, where there is nothing scheduled? Is there protected time for families and members of the family to just rest and be? Or to participate in something that hasn't already been planned?* It's a time to be free of all the "should" and "have to" tasks and to simply rest. It's a great time of connection in families, as they are free to be creative, and do things that aren't demanded of them.

Whether we call it margin, "white space," or something similar, it is essentially the same concept. It is the act of creating space that is free of busyness.

I see this task of creating space and margin as being very different from observing the Sabbath. In Genesis 2:3 we read:

Then God blessed the seventh day and made it holy,
because on it he rested from all the work of creating that he
had done.

Sabbath keeping is something that was designed to be a
part of us by our Creator. It is a day where we rest in the work
that God has already done. It is a laying down of our wants,
demands, and activities to be content in what God has
already accomplished in our lives. It is a discipline of
acknowledging that I don't have to produce or do something
in order to be right before God. It's an act of being versus
doing. This is reflected in the New Testament, especially at
Jesus' baptism in Mark 1:9–11, where I mentioned earlier
that Jesus' identity is grounded in His being in relationship
with His Father, and not in His doing. Author and theologian
Marva Dawn in her poignant book *Keeping the Sabbath
Wholly* remarks,

> Consequently, Sabbath days—when we don't have to do
> anything—can release us from the anxiety that accompa-
> nies our work (as long as we don't add to our stress by tak-
> ing on too many Sunday responsibilities). Furthermore, our
> false need to be productive (even in the church) builds
> stress, especially when we find ourselves unable to meet
> our exorbitant expectations.[4]

Creating space is something that we do on top of Sabbath
keeping. These are built-in times that are focused on rest,
and allowing the creativity in ourselves and our families to

come to fruition. Many people over-schedule their lives with busyness and activities like sports and hobbies because they have somewhere lost the ability to just *be* with others outside of having to be busy and perform. Theologian Henri Nouwen insightfully remarks that

> Occupation and not empty space is what most of us are looking for. When we are not occupied we become restless. We even become fearful when we do not know what we will do the next hour, the next day or the next year.... We are so afraid of open spaces and empty places that we occupy them with our minds even before we are there. Our worries and concerns are expressions of our inability to leave unresolved questions unresolved and open-ended situations open-ended.[5]

I believe we observe the Sabbath because that is something we do to foster our relationship with God, and to declare that we are dependent upon Him, rather than ourselves. And we protect space in our lives because that is something we do to foster our relationship not only with God, but with ourselves, and with those we live, work, and play with.

When an individual or family loses the ability to foster a Sabbath, or create space in their lives, I know that there are usually deeper things at work. Often individuals and families are afraid to just be by themselves, or with one another, without something planned to do. Nouwen writes, "Empty space tends to create fear. As long as our minds, hearts and hands are occupied we can avoid confronting the painful questions, to which we never gave much attention and which we do not want to surface."[6] That fear and hesitation points to the very need to create space and practice a Sabbath. When we have Sabbath and space in our lives, we are free to face our anxiety, which may be one of the reasons so many people avoid it.

Living Within Our Limitations

Events such as marriage, the birth of a child, death, divorce, moving to a new city, or a transition into a new career are powerful events in one's life. They are events that often bring into focus our limitations in life, quickly eliminating many choices and options, but also bringing better clarity and focus. The existential psychiatrist Irvin Yalom refers to these events as "boundary experiences"[7] because of their ability to bring a person to a sense of awareness of what is happening in their life.

We live in a culture that says you can do anything and everything you want to do, and it provides you with choices and possibilities that are endless. That creates a lot of anxiety for a lot of people. But as we embrace our possibilities we must also live within limits to what we can do and achieve, regardless of our ambition or drive. Many see this as a hindrance to our lives, but living within limits creates freedom for us. Living within these limits can help people reimagine their anxiety in healthy ways, channeling it as a source of growth, rather than a debilitating feeling.

To hearken back to Kierkegaard's earlier words about

Adam in the garden of Eden, it is precisely this tension between living in the freedom of possibility, and the freedom of limits, that God uses to transform our lives. God defined both Adam's freedom and his limits, and it is that tension that he was called to live in (Genesis 2:16–17). We can, therefore, listen to our anxiety and stay in that tension as God is shaping us, or we can ignore anxiety's call upon our lives and continue to stuff it below the surface, or bury it in a flurry of activity.

Sometimes having limited options and choices is true freedom because it clarifies things. Limits help a person focus on something more intently, rather than always playing around with what choice to make. Sociologist Barry Schwartz in his book *The Paradox of Choice* writes about the anxiety that accompanies even buying jeans these days:

> At this point, choice no longer liberates, but debilitates. . . .
> But clinging tenaciously to all the choices available to us
> contributes to bad decisions, to anxiety, stress, and
> dissatisfaction—even to clinical depression.[8]

This anxiety over choice is experienced by people in all stages of life, but I especially see this struggle with young adults, primarily those who are making the transition from college into the "real world"/"working world." There are often so many choices and options before them that they quickly become paralyzed out of fear of making the wrong choice.

Part of being human is accepting our limits along with our potential, and living within that tension. With each new transition in life I have had to wrestle with the number of possibilities available to me and make some choices—choices that limit other things that could have been. With every Yes that I declare, a No is declared as well. We are always renouncing one thing in favor of the other thing. Many people cannot accept this, constantly believing they can do everything, which leads to burnout, depression, and a workaholic mentality, to name a few.

When each of my children was born, I instantly realized that there were some things in my life that I could no longer attend to or attempt. I was faced with an ever-increasing limitation of time with a growing family. But instead of seeing that as a hindrance, I realized what a beautiful thing it is when something like a family can help one place limitations on their life, and by doing so bring sharper clarity to what is truly important, and to what truly needs attending to. It is a gift.

Now that I have cleared my plate of many things, the things that do remain can be focused on with more intensity and purpose than ever before. In essence, I can be more intentional about the things I am now focused on. These are my limits, and with these limits comes a freedom that no longer leaves me treading water in a sea of options, fearful that I might make the wrong choice, or limit myself to all the other possibilities.

This anxiety is the tool that God uses to continually shape me, allowing me to navigate the tension between the freedom He gives me and the limits He has placed before me.

I am reminded of a beautiful passage by Parker Palmer in

his remarkable book *Let Your Life Speak: Listening for the Voice of Vocation:*

> Our deepest calling is to grow into our own authentic self-hood, whether or not it conforms to some image of who we ought to be. As we do so, we will not only find the joy that every human being seeks—we will also find our path of authentic service in the world. True vocation joins self and service, as Frederick Buechner asserts when he defines vocation as "the place where your deep gladness meets the world's deep need."[9]

As we work to achieve a healthy balance between our God-given potential and God-given limitations, we will move toward fulfillment and peace, and acquire the internal resources to bless those around us.

Discussion Questions

1. If anxiety can often point to an area of one's life where there is the need for a boundary, what boundary needs to be established in your life?

2. What is one thing you can do today to create more margin in your life?

3. What keeps you from practicing the Sabbath?

4. What are some limits that have been placed in your life that you may be ignoring and that may be resulting in more anxiety?

Exercises

1. Take out a piece of paper, drawing two vertical lines of equal length, creating three columns. In column one, write from top to bottom the various stages of life that you have transitioned through (for example, childhood, junior high, high school, college, young adult, career, marriage, parenting, etc.). In column two, next to each transitional stage, identify one limit that was placed upon you by necessity in that stage of life. In column three, identify one freedom/possibility that was given to you as a result.

2. As you look at the three-column chart, reflect on where anxiety might have been present in those stages of life and how God might have been using it to help you grow.

Prayer

God, thank You that You have given me freedom in my life. Please help me know where to establish healthy boundaries, in order that I may create space, practice Sabbath, and live a thriving life within the limits You have set before me.

chapter eight

Relational Refinement

"Being free means 'being free for the other',
because I am bound to the other.
Only in relationship with the other am I free."[1]

DIETRICH BONHOEFFER,
Creation and Fall/Temptation: Two Biblical Studies

From the outset of creation God designed that we should live together in community. We see this communal yearning in God's creation beginning in Genesis 1:26 where God says, "Let us make man in our image, in our likeness." It's a beautiful image of the Godhead—Father, Son, and Holy Spirit —relationally interacting with one another in this trinitarian community, often referred to as *perichoresis*.[2] It is out of that divine community that Adam and Eve emerged and from which you and I were birthed. The text says in Genesis 1:27:

> So God created mankind in his own image,
> in the image of God he created them;
> male and female he created them.

The blueprint for you and me is that we are not to be alone (Genesis 2:18), but that we should live in community with one another. It is in that community of others that we reach our fullest potential as God's created beings.

But things don't always go the way that we hope for or anticipate. We see that from the beginning Adam and Eve got pulled into their own fears and unhealthy ways of interacting with one another. Though the text doesn't explicitly use the word *anxiety*, a feeling of anxiousness is present. There is great shame in their act of eating the forbidden fruit, an act that drives them away from God and into a place of being distant and alone. And there in that lonely place anxiety festered and permeated their actions. Adam and Eve hid from God, blamed each other, and tried to cover up what they had done. It sounds awfully similar to how you and I are when we let anxiety pervade our lives and move away from each other, rather than toward one another.

This movement of coming close and distancing was very present in the early years of my marriage. I found myself wanting my wife to be close to me. I wanted to feel that sense of dependency upon her, and her dependency upon me. But often, even without noticing, I would find myself moving away from her, desiring to establish some type of autonomy. It was almost as if I had drawn a line in the sand, like the historic character from which my middle name, Travis,[3] was taken. Though I did not verbally communicate this to Heather, what I was saying inside was, "I'm not giving up anymore of myself to be in relationship with you. I can do this on my own. This is all of me you are getting." I lived in a state of semi-anxiety, fearing that I might be swallowed up in this relationship.

Relational Refinement

At times it seems like there are warring factions within us. One of the factions has a great yearning to escape and be alone and to see if it can survive on its own. We want to be independent and feel a sense of accomplishment in knowing that we navigated various life transitions without anyone's help. Yet, there is another faction that desires to be with others and that craves the sense of belonging that comes with being in relational community with other people. We want to be able to depend on others and we hope that others can also depend on us.

This inner turmoil often creates a lot of anxiety as we feel pulled between the two places and we struggle to figure out a proper balance for our lives.

But in the struggle with my anxiety, I slowly realized that I was created to be in relationship with others and now I had found its fullest meaning in my marriage to Heather. I couldn't figure out why marriage was so tough, and why an intimate relationship with another human being could cause so much anxiety. I like the words of marriage and sex therapist David Schnarch in his book *Passionate Marriage* when he refers to marriage as "people growing machines."[4] This relationship that I now found myself in was designed by God, not only for me to experience an intimate connection with another person, but to help me to grow up and become a more mature human being. Terry Hargrave writes, "one of the basic philosophies I have about all relationships is that they require us to grow up a little and learn more about ourselves."[5] I might add that they often require us to grow up more than a little—perhaps a great deal!

I believe that one of the reasons that God wired us for connection with others is because it is in relationships with others that we are truly refined. All relationships have the possibility of refining us more and more to reflect the image of God, helping us reach our fullest potential that we could not otherwise achieve alone.

This refinement occurs when you and I are in friendships with other people.

This refinement occurs when you and I are interacting in community with others.

This refinement occurs in our families.

This refinement occurs in marriage, but also occurs in our singleness and in the relationships we maintain.

And it also occurs in our parenting, where we are constantly being refined by our interactions with our children.

Relational refinement is a scary process filled with much anxiety as we bounce between the image we often try to project of ourselves, and the true reality that others see when we are in relationship with them. A true relationship doesn't allow you to be someone other than who you are. I love the apostle Paul's words in 1 Corinthians 13:11–12, where he writes,

> When I was a child, I talked like a child, I thought like a child, I reasoned like a child. When I became a man, I put the ways of childhood behind me. For now we see only a reflection as in a mirror; then we shall see face to face. Now I know in part; then I shall know fully, even as I am fully known.

Relational Refinement

Relationships help us grow up from being a child into being an adult. Apart from relationships, we tend to project and reflect back in our own mirrors the image we desire to see of ourselves. But it is in relationships that we see who we really are, which challenges us to look at ourselves, face our anxieties, and grow in ways we never could have imagined. Relationships, both earthly and heavenly, are our greatest opportunity to be fully known.

I first saw Heather in February of 2003 at a David Crowder concert that I helped host at our church. It was a very brief encounter, but I began to admire her from afar while looking for opportunities to engage her in person whenever possible. Each time we talked with one another, I tried to put my best foot forward, projecting the image of this strong and confident guy that I hoped she could see. I think we each did that in our encounters and as we moved into a dating relationship. The desire to be seen in a positive light only intensifies as the relationship continues. This sort of charade often goes on for most of dating, but eventually the illusion is shattered in marriage where our partner may no longer buy into the image that we have so desperately tried to convey.

But it's a freeing experience to let go of the anxiety of trying to be someone else, and finally come to grips with who we are. To be able to do that in the context of a relationship and a community is both a humbling and a freeing experience. It was only apropos that the young adult community that I participated and met Heather in was called the Foundry, and their worship nights the Refinery. Both are places of refinement, and both acted as agents of that process in my own life.

Though we are wired for connection, we often without notice, very subtly, resist the refining process that relationships and community call us toward. Anytime we start to feel anxious, or we start to believe that we have been found out for who we really are, we often do just like Adam and Eve did, and flee into hiding. To be faced with our true reality in front of others is a humbling and terrifying experience, as we face the anxiety of whether or not we will be accepted for who we are, rather than for the image that we tried so hard to make appealing to others.

This is one of the reasons that many relationships and marriages end up with infidelities and affairs. When our partner no longer sees or buys into the image that we have tried so hard to polish, we escape by finding someone else who will see us that way. And as long as that person can maintain the illusion along with us, that affair or new relationship will continue. But once the illusion is shattered, many escape to find another relationship, starting the whole process over again.

This is also one of the reasons that many people go from church community to church community, shopping for the church that best meets their needs. What they fail to realize is that no church will ever meet their needs, nor is a church designed to do that. Rather, underneath, the person is really anxious for others in community to see them for who they really are. This anxiety often propels young adults, couples, and families from one community to the next.

An authentic human connection occurs when we can stand in front of others and can feel their acceptance and love and grace in spite of any flaws or differences that may exist. When we don't have to put on our masks and try to pretend to be someone else, that is a truly freeing experience. But to get to that place takes work and it takes courage to go down that path that is fraught with so much relational anxiety.

When we can stand face-to-face with another human being in all of our anxiety, and we don't have to try to run or hide from it, that is the beginning of a true relational connection. A primary example of the type of relational anxiety that occurs in so many relationships involves the area of conflict. Many communities, friends, and families do anything to avoid conflict. They don't face the anxiety that the conflict arouses, but instead try to hide from it or push it down below the surface. When we do this we can never truly be ourselves. I like what my friend and marriage therapist Todd Sandel says, "Conflict is the channel through which we grow." When we finally stop running from our true selves, and face our anxiety, we are presented with the possibility to achieve growth like we have never experienced. And the relationships that we are in are just the refining friction that we need to help shape us more into God's image.

Belonging to the Body

The life transitions and the wilderness wanderings that many of us find ourselves in can be terrifying places. These are the frightening places where many of us often feel most alone. But I'm struck by the fact that in Exodus 17:1 the Israelites went out together as a congregation. God may have called out individuals to lead (like Moses and Aaron) and to step out alone at times in the journey, but it was a movement of an entire community of people. When our anxiety is heightened and we are called forth into new territory, we want to go out with others as a group of people.

One of my favorite movies growing up as a kid was *Lone Wolf McQuade* starring Chuck Norris as Texas Ranger J. J. McQuade. The title alone asserts what we have come to believe wholeheartedly in our culture, and it has seeped into our Christian and church cultures as well. The message is that we don't need others, but can go out alone, as a lone wolf. It makes for a great movie and Norris was more than capable of taking on an entire army of arms dealers, as well as taking out *Kung Fu* legend David Carradine in the final scene of the movie. Chuck Norris may be able to journey through the wilderness alone (insert your favorite Chuck Norris quip here), but God did not design us that way.

In the wilderness, we go out together as a congregation, a community of people, dependent upon God and one another in our anxiety-filled travel. This does not mean that we don't ever do anything by ourselves, or don't need our time alone, but it does mean that when we are accompanied by a community of people, we are more likely to receive the support and encouragement it takes for us to survive in the wilderness. When I traveled and lived in Guatemala, for all practical purposes I took the journey alone, but I was never truly alone because of the community of people who were a part of that journey. Parker Palmer reminds us that

Community does not necessarily mean living face-to-face with others; rather, it means never losing the awareness that we are connected to each other. It is not about the presence of other people—it is about being fully open to the reality of relationship, whether or not we are alone.[6]

I had friends and family back at home who were supporting me on this trip and who were in continual prayer for me. I went down for the initial month with a couple of old college friends, and I would continue to make new friends along the way. I was alone, but God had provided a community of people to journey along with me.

The importance of Christian community was brought home to me in the spring of 2007 while I was traveling with college students down the Rio Negro River in Brazil on a mission trip. Approximately one hour before our church service began, one of the missionary leaders suddenly asked, "Will you preach tonight?"

"Yes," I said quickly and anxiously.

My fast reply was probably a mixture of never being able to say no, but also wanting to face my anxieties. I've always reflected back on my promise to God that if He gave me an opportunity to speak, I would take it no matter the anxiety. And for the most part I have always tried to face my anxiety by accepting opportunities to speak unless there was a valid reason to say no. Anxiety was not a valid reason.

I began to prepare a sermon that I would be giving in less than an hour to a Brazilian church in the port we had just pulled into. In that moment of anxiousness all my feelings of being abandoned and alone came creeping up and what I really wanted to do was just head back to the boat and hide out for the rest of the night.

But instead, I tried to really stay engaged with what God was doing in our midst and I told Him that if this sermon was going to turn out decently at all, then He would have to perform a miracle and essentially speak for me. One of the things I do when I get anxious is withdraw, not in order to hide, but to find a place of calmness within me. In that place of calm aboard that large boat I began to have this beautiful image of the people on board in cramped quarters but working together as a cohesive unit.

I get anxious and feel a pit in my stomach just recalling that story. During that mission trip as we slowly wound our way down that huge river, our group of twenty-three students, and the group of twenty-three boat crew, quickly became a community of forty-six people. As I thought about how God brought together that community of people from varying countries and backgrounds, put us together in tight quarters on a boat for eight days, I began to see the refining process that took place among us. It reminded me of the apostle Paul's words in 1 Corinthians 12:12–14; 27, which is the text I preached from that night:

> Just as a body, though one, has many parts, but all its many parts form one body, so it is with Christ. For we were all baptized by one Spirit so as to form one body—whether Jews or Gentiles, slave or free—and we were all given the

one Spirit to drink. Even so the body is not made up of one part but of many.

Now you are the body of Christ, and each one of you is a part of it.

It was because we were a body, belonging to God and to one another, that we could see and use each and every one of our individual gifts that God had given us. Apart from community and each other, our gifts have no meaning. Perhaps we would never have even known our gifts at all if we had not been refined in the process of living life together in a close community.

I remember in particular one client who had come to see me because of his growing anxiety that was slowly turning into a debilitating force. We worked on his anxiety for a long time, continually wondering and seeking what God was saying to him in his anxiety. Then one day the client came into my office declaring that he had discovered what God had created him to do. His discovery came in the midst of a community of people who were unintentionally helping to refine him. It was amazing to see his unhealthy anxiety dissipate at the discovery of his gifts in that community. Dietrich Bonhoeffer, who at the age of twenty-one wrote his dissertation *Sanctorum Communio* (the communion of saints), says this about community:

God does not desire a history of individual human beings, but the history of the human community. Nor does God want a community which absorbs the individual into itself, but a community of human beings. In God's sight community and individual are present in the same moment and rest upon one another.[7]

Boundaries in Marriage and Relationships: When the Two Become Three

How we answer the question "Where do I begin and end in relationship to you" is very important. Because in that question we are wondering how we can possibly be in relationship with someone else without losing our own sense of self-worth and identity. This process is known as differentiation and as David Schnarch describes it,

> involves balancing two basic life forces: the drive for individuality and the drive for togetherness. Individuality propels us to follow our own directives, to be on our own, to create a unique identity. Togetherness pushes us to follow the directives of others, to be part of the group. When these two life forces for individuality and togetherness are expressed in balanced, healthy ways, the result is a meaningful relationship that doesn't deteriorate into emotional fusion.[8]

Everyone in a relationship knows what this feels like. We have all been in that position of wanting people that we care about to be close to us, but also at times wanting to get some space from them. We create this "pull close and push away" dynamic in relationships when we experience anxiety and are unable to manage and soothe it on our own. What we are left with then is the belief that if I just push people away when I feel anxious, even if for a short time, then that will solve my problems. But pushing people away because we can't manage our own anxiety is actually an avoidance of the real issue, rather than a healthy interaction in pursuit of establishing boundaries:

> Another definition of differentiation is the ability to maintain a clear sense of self in close proximity to a partner. The higher your level of differentiation, the closer you can get to your partner, because you're not afraid of losing yourself. It gives you a solid but permeable self, which allows you to make a decision to be influenced and to change (as opposed to having to change to stay on good terms with your partner). At high levels of differentiation, what your partner wants in his/her life becomes as important to you as what you want.[9]

Even as I write these words I can't but help reflect on my first year of marriage with Heather.

It was very amazing. And it was very hard. If you ask her I'm sure she would tell you the same.

At some point during our first few months of marriage I found myself wondering if Heather and I could make this marriage work. My wonderment wasn't about our commitment to one another, or whether or not we should stay or not stay married. Instead, my questioning was based in my fear that I was losing myself in the marriage relationship. It felt like I was losing control of my life and that there was this other person with input into how things should be done. At times, the situation felt like a threat to who I was trying to be. I know Heather had the same fears as well. We just didn't know how to express it then.

So when I felt like I was losing myself, I would begin to feel anxious and I would tend to just withdraw from the relationship, somehow believing that by distancing myself I could hold onto me. That's what I had been doing for the thirty years leading up to our marriage. This pattern of interaction for me didn't have its roots in our marriage (remember, we learn our ways of coping prior to marriage, most often in our families of origin), but it certainly came to the forefront in our marriage in an intense manner. I remember reading Mike Mason's wonderful book *The Mystery of Marriage* years before my own marriage and I was always struck by his idea that marriage is something of a surprising and alarming invasion upon us. These words only began to make sense to me after getting married, which is really the crucible where we learn to both hang onto ourselves and to one another.

So there we were—the two of us. We were madly in love with each other, but also fearful of one another. Fearful that to be together also meant losing parts of ourselves. In that first year of marriage, Heather and I created a pain cycle that kept us in a continual pattern of anger, distancing, and shutting down from one another. These were all behaviors that kept us from facing our anxieties, and learning to establish healthy marriage boundaries. We thought that space would allow us to maintain a clear sense of self while also learning to be in relationship with one another, but our pattern looked more like separating and moving apart. We were coming close and pulling apart, but never truly learning to be differentiated from one another in a healthy manner. In fact, this can only take place in the refining fires of our relational anxiety as we stay close to one another through our conflicts.

I can't clearly recall one defining moment in our marriage when we began to face our anxieties together. Rather, it was a combination of several things. I was in graduate school at the time working on my masters in marital and family therapy. Talk about anxiety provoking! Every day I would learn about what ideal, healthy, relational functioning looked like, but I didn't think we had it, and that created ongoing anxiety.

But one of the saving graces about the graduate school training was that the state of California encouraged its marriage and family therapy students to go to therapy during the program. And the Fuller Theological Seminary community also encouraged therapy, so that we would not only grow ourselves, but better understand our clients' experience of being in therapy. So every week for two years I went to therapy and tried to face my anxiety. And every week I was challenged more and more to take a hard look at myself, which is the only person I actually have any control over. I was in the process of learning the most important gift that I could give Heather, and that any of us can give our partner. That is, the ability to self-soothe our own anxiety.

Every day I worked on learning how to cope with my own anxiety in a healthy way. This was my issue and it was something I needed to take responsibility for in our marriage. It was not something I should expect Heather to do for me. Nothing is as needy in a relationship as expecting your partner to constantly take care of your needs and bandage you up when you feel wounded. That is truly disempowering for both people and doesn't promote healthy relational boundaries.

The beautiful thing about taking responsibility for your own anxiety, and the actions that follow it, is that it creates the space for your partner to also confront themselves. Partners cannot confront themselves and face their own anxieties when they constantly have to rush in and prop the other person up. I faced my own anxieties because I needed to. Regardless of what Heather did or didn't do, my integrity demanded that I work on myself. But the fruit of that is that it gave space for Heather to work on her own issues as well. The result is that you have two people in a marriage both taking responsibility for their own actions. That is a beautiful thing and transforms the unhealthy cycle into something truly life-giving.

Our Christian culture creates a lot of anxiety when it comes to marriage and being in relationship with one another. I think there is a misconception out there that being married means giving up ourselves for the other person. We read Genesis 2:24 ("For this reason a man will leave his father and mother and be united to his wife, and they will become one flesh") and we know we are commanded to be one flesh, but surely that doesn't mean losing yourself in the process. And we live in a Christian culture that usually expects the female to give herself up for her husband, though the text seems to demand that the husband is the one who leaves his father and mother, essentially giving up his sense of self and his familial relational identity.

But is it really an either/or command?

Does being in relationship necessarily mean that we give ourselves up?

What does it look like for us to be in relationship with one another and to hold on to ourselves while we also hold on to our partners?

What does it really look like for the two to become one?

The marriage and family therapist Terry Hargrave talks about the creation of an "us-ness"[10] when two get married and become one. It's not a merging of two identities into one person, a merging that requires each person to lose themselves to become one. Rather, it is two distinct beings forming a third identity—"us-ness." My wife and I have very different interests and what I'm realizing now is that marriage did not require that we give ourselves up in order for us to be in relationship with one another; rather, it demanded that we maintain who we are in order that we form this third person in our midst. We are three distinct beings, yet we are still one.

I love the words of the Bohemian-Austrian poet Rainer Maria Rilke in his powerful book, *Letters to a Young Poet*:

> Love is at first not anything that means merging, giving over, and uniting with another (for what would a union be of something unclarified and unfinished, still subordinate?), it is a high inducement to the individual to ripen, to become

something in himself for another's sake, it is a great exacting claim upon him, something that chooses him out and calls him to vast things.[11]

In our fear of being swallowed up in a relationship we can lose sight of the beautiful interrelating that occurs between two people. We don't need to distance ourselves, nor do we need to merge ourselves in order to become one. Distancing and merging are both ways of managing our anxiety in relationship to one another.

But there is a different way.

There is a way to be fully yourself, while being fully connected in a relationship to another human being.

There is another way that the two become one.

I love the account in Mark 1:9–11 where the gospel writer paints this beautiful scene, which we've noted before:

> At that time Jesus came from Nazareth in Galilee and was baptized by John in the Jordan. Just as Jesus was coming up out of the water, he saw heaven being torn open and the Spirit descending on him like a dove. And a voice came from heaven: "You are my Son, whom I love; with you I am well pleased."

Father, Son, and Spirit together in one scene. Fully one, but fully three. Each are fully themselves, while still being in relationship with one another.

If we are made in the image of God (Genesis 1:26), then we are to reflect that image. We are to reflect the same type of intermingling that we witness between the three, but distinct, members of the Godhead. This relating exemplifies a relationship that gives full freedom to each of its members while still maintaining its relational unity. So as people who were fashioned in the image of God, one of the most grace-giving and freeing things we can do for others that we are in relationship with is to create space that allows each individual to flourish in the relationship. Anything that snuffs out this freedom and demands a forfeit of one's self in relationship is neither healthy nor biblical.

When we are in a healthy relationship with others we are able to maintain our identity and our sense of self, a self that is not dependent upon other people. Some of the most anxious people around are those who are in a constant state of pursuit as they try to solicit the affirmation or validation that they need from others. Without this "other validation" they will lose a sense of who they really are and become stuck in a place of anxiety.

In contrast, a Christian's sense of self is not dependent upon others, but is dependent upon ourselves—though not us alone. It is a dependency rooted in our relationship with Jesus Christ. Christ is the validation that gives meaning to who we are and that allows us as individuals to self-validate, rather than other-validate, which means always seeking out others in order to feel good about ourselves.

The early years in our marriage were characterized by my need for Heather to constantly validate and affirm me. I wanted to hear "You are the best husband" all the time. I wanted her to know how lucky she was to be married to me.

I wanted her to constantly affirm my pastoral work and the gifts that I believed I had. That was a no-win situation for Heather, and really for any of us involved in relationships. Even wanting Heather to constantly meet my needs was really a desire for "other validation," a validation which pulls us away from being dependent upon God for who we are and how we feel about ourselves, and places our dependency upon our partner to meet all of our needs.

As we come to terms with our anxiety, it is important for us to understand that part of God's work of helping us re-imagine anxiety takes place in community, especially within the body of Christ, made possible because of Jesus' resurrection. In our encounter with others He refines us and gives us the opportunity to grow in the process. Eugene Peterson makes an important statement about this necessity of resurrection and community, which I conclude with:

> Jesus did not raise himself; he was raised. And we do not raise ourselves; we are raised. . . . It is critical that we get inside this and make it our own, critical that we realize not just that the resurrection happened but that it happens. . . . It happens, we do not make it happen. . . . The more we practice resurrection the less we are on our own by ourselves, for we find that this resurrection that is so intensely and relationally personal in Father, Son, and Spirit at the same time plunges us into relationships with brothers and sisters we never knew we had: we are in community whether we like it or not.[12]

Discussion Questions

1. How do you understand the distinction in community between feeling the freedom to be yourself, but allowing others to refine you in the process in order that you may become more fully yourself?

2. Can you think of a relationship that caused a lot of anxiety for you? What was the source of that anxiety? Did you experience an anxious tension between desiring to be together, but also separate? Describe that anxiety.

3. How might the model of the Trinity be a model for how we relate to others in our relationships?

Exercise

Self-soothing is one's ability to properly regulate their emotions and responses, especially in relationship to others. As you interact with others, practice being aware of your own anxiety. As you become aware of your anxiety, experiment with self-soothing and holding on to or working through that anxiety, rather than reacting. As you self-soothe you should practice healthy self-soothing techniques, because unhealthy self-soothing techniques often lead not only to more anxiety but destructive behaviors in a relationship (for example, excessive drinking, drugs, pornography, etc.). For one month, experiment with being aware of your relational anxiety and practice self-soothing—maintaining awareness that God is the One who ultimately meets all of your needs.

Prayer

> *God, I thank You that You have created me in Your image, and in that image You have created me to be relational. I ask that You give me the courage to participate in community, interacting in the lives of others as You refine us.*

Living Life
as a Stutterer

"There is one within me who is more myself than my self."

SAINT AUGUSTINE

W ould you be interested in being the speaker for our young adult retreat in October?"

That was the question from Keenan Barber as we were talking on the phone. It was already the final days of August, 2010, and the retreat was less than two months away. The original speaker had fallen through and Keenan, who is the young adult pastor at Bel Air Presbyterian Church, was curious if I would be willing to do four talks over the October 15–17 weekend at the Forest Home camp in Ojai, California.

"Yes, I would love to be the speaker, but let's talk this through so that you feel like I'm the right speaker for your young adult group."

My response was one of the ways that I walked that fine line of trying to manage my anxiety, making sure I took risks to speak, but also giving someone every opportunity to decide I wasn't the right speaker for their group. At least if Keenan decided I wasn't the right guy, then it wouldn't feel as much like I was dodging my own anxiety. It was a way for me to feel like I was taking responsibility for my life without being overtly intentional. And as we explored more explicitly what it would look like for me to be the speaker that weekend, I began to hear that voice again, the one that had spoken to me in the spring of 1996.

The voice was the same, but we had been developing a more intimate relationship over the last fourteen years. It spoke softly, but just as firmly. "Rhett, take this speaking opportunity and I will be there with you. I know you are scared. I know it's been a long time since you have spoken at a retreat, but face your fears, and I will walk alongside of you. Face your anxiety and I will grow you in the process. You will come out a different person."

I had not been asking God for opportunities to speak, which were situations that were fearful for me. But God knew, as I did, that I needed to take more risks in order to not let my anxiety take control of me, and for my faith to not grow stagnant in the process. When I resigned from Bel Air Presbyterian Church and finished up my last day in June of 2008, I had begun the process of removing myself from preaching, something that I had been doing almost every week for the last six years. I liked where I was at in life. I liked being in the counseling office one-on-one with individuals, couples, and families. I liked teaching a monthly parenting class at Highland Park Presbyterian Church in Dallas. Those things were different than speaking in front of others. I was comfortable and content with my varying roles, and I liked that my anxiety seemed to be lying dormant for a season.

That month and a half leading up to the young adult retreat was one of the most stressful times I have ever experienced before a speaking event. It seemed as if the nights flew by without sleep and the days dragged by with worry. Though this may sound overly dramatic, I felt like a man with a death sentence. I wasn't going to be physically dead because of the retreat, but I had done a good job convincing myself that I would stutter my way through the entire event. I was certain that I would walk away that weekend with my head down and a cloud of shame hanging over me. Those early experiences in childhood of being humiliated in front of my classmates as I tried to read were still floating around in my mind.

Once anxiety manages to get a grip on our lives we are forever locked in a battle of fighting those fears and negative beliefs we have about ourselves, our choices, and all the future possibilities that lie ahead of us. But if we can beat anxiety one time, just one time, a new battle begins to take place. We go into that new battle with anxiety knowing that we have beaten it once. There is a sense of confidence that we can beat it again. It had been a long time since I felt like I had won that battle with my fears. The funny thing is that no one else knew that there was this battle raging on inside of me. God knew. My wife knew. But Keenan didn't know. His young adults didn't know. Sometimes when we face our fears it is a battle that only we know about.

Routine Therapy Checkup

On October 20, 2010, I went in for what I would call a routine therapy checkup. Routine because I didn't really feel like I had the energy to work on much of anything worthwhile, and I didn't expect the therapist to press me too hard before my big weekend.

As I sat down on his couch he started the session the way he usually did by asking, "So what do you want to work on today?"

"I don't know," was my response.

But as I sat there I figured I had better use the time that I have wisely, so I said, "I'm speaking this weekend and I'm just nervous. Actually, I have a lot of anxiety about the whole situation."

"Were you ever made fun of as a child growing up?" he asked me.

"No," was my immediate response. Didn't he know I had lots of great friends growing up?

"Did you ever find yourself the center of attention?" he asked this time.

As I was wondering where he was going with this line of questioning, I had a flash of memory light up in my head. And then I remembered that I was made fun of as a kid, but I had tried to block those memories out. I remembered being in the classroom in elementary school and kids making fun of my stuttering. I remembered that feeling, feeling like I was the center of everyone's attention because of my inability to read well.

"Rhett, I want you to close your eyes," my therapist said to me. I loved closing my eyes in session and having him walk me through some exercises. I always felt relaxed and non-anxious afterward.

"I want you to imagine being in fifth grade again. And I want you to imagine walking back into your class the first day back after your mom died. As you stand there in the class-room I want you, the adult Rhett, to just imagine the fifth-grade Rhett as he enters that class. And as he walks into that classroom I want you to look around at the faces of all your classmates. That must have been a very hard time—you feel-ing like the center of attention. Your teacher probably talked to your classmates about your mom dying, and they probably didn't know how to respond either. Rhett, I want you to look around the classroom and try to remember various faces of your classmates and what they looked like. Imagine what they must have been feeling. Don't tell me, but I want you to imagine what advice you, the adult Rhett, would give the fifth-grade Rhett on that day. Tell him, but not out loud so that I can hear."

This exercise continued for a while and then very slowly he had me open my eyes. As we sat there in his office I could feel the power of that moment emanating between the two of us.

He then asked, "What did the adult Rhett tell the fifth-grade Rhett?"

I know this conversation may sound strange to many of you, especially those of you who may have never been to therapy, or may have never walked through such an exercise. But what happened next was life-changing for me.

"I told him that he was going to be okay. I told him that everything would work out okay. I told him that I knew things were real tough, but he just needed to hang in there. I told him that he would be all right." And then the tears that were slowly welling up in my eyes could no longer be held at bay and I began sobbing like I have possibly never sobbed since the death of my mom.

It's hard to explain what happened, but there was a sense of peace that God brought over me that day that I had never quite experienced before. I walked out of the therapy room knowing that I would defeat my dragon of anxiety and that it would never have a stranglehold on my life again. I wish someone had been able to tell me growing up that life was going to be okay. That I was going to be okay. That I was going to make it. I had been held in bondage for so many years in my anxiety that I really never knew if I was going to be okay, or if I was going to make it. But I knew now that I was.

I was a thirty-five-year-old grown man sitting in my therapist's office sobbing like an uncontrollable child. It was one of the most freeing moments that I have ever experienced. As I sat there I was amazed that events that began as early in my life as age six had exerted such strong control over my life in terms of my feelings and behaviors. I began to realize that all those years I had allowed anxiety to get a stronger hold over my life. There had been moments of intervention, where I leaned into it, and allowed God to bring good out of it. But anxiety was still in a battle to exert more control over my life than I wanted.

Speaking Freely

On October 15, 2010, at approximately 9:30 p.m., I began my first talk for the Foundry young adult retreat. This was the culmination of my decision nearly two months before to face my fears and speak. And as I began speaking, I realized that for probably the first time in my life, God did beautiful things with my anxiety when I turned toward Him. By doing so it was a moment for God to be glorified in my weakness. I realized that my weakness was no longer about me being someone who was a failure or not good enough, or that because I felt weak I had somehow been left alone and abandoned by God. Rather, as each confident word came rolling out of my mouth, I knew that God truly was taking my anxiety and using it for His good.

I know that you may be struggling with anxiety right now and the last thing you want to do is face it. I know that in those fearful moments it is almost impossible to believe that God can take your weakness and use it to do great and wonderful things. That is okay. I have been there. All I am asking is that you just begin the journey of imagining what it might look like for God to use your anxiety for good. You don't have to go out and face your anxiety head-on tomorrow. You don't have to go deliver a talk, or make that move, or change careers. You just need to enter that stage-to-stage journey that God is calling you on. Take it a day at a time. Take it a step at a time.

My anxiety has not disappeared. In fact, every talk that I delivered that retreat weekend took all the energy I had to lean into God and allow Him to use my weakness for His glory. That was hard. I wanted to be able to defeat and fix it myself. But that is not my role. God was just asking me to join Him in that process, where it was my responsibility to face my fears, and when I did that, He transformed my anxiety in ways that I couldn't have imagined.

So start today with one simple step.

What is causing you anxiety?

What keeps you up at night, tossing and turning?

What is that one thing that you feel God is calling you to do, but that you are fearful of?

Slowly . . . very slowly . . . turn and face it. And as you do, I promise that God will be there to use your anxiety for His good.

Reaching for Help

"As I began to share what was really going on with my friends and coworkers, many times those same people would share with me their own struggles with anxiety, depression or other issues.

I realize when other people share their struggles with me, it builds an instant bridge of trust. I know I can talk with them because they've walked in my shoes. It also makes a 'me too' moment. I think it was Rob Bell who said the words 'me too' are the two most comforting words in the English language.

Again, just starting that conversation and allowing others the permission to share knowing they will be welcomed with grace and trust and love —unconditionally, is why I am so passionate about talking about these things."[1]

ANNE JACKSON, *Interview with the author*

Last summer, for some inexplicable reason, my wife and I became captivated by the television programming on the Animal Planet network. If you have ever watched the station then you probably know what I'm talking about. Some of the content of the shows was so disturbing and surreal that it was hard to look sometimes. One night we were watching the show *Infested* and there was a story about a family who had bought and moved into a home in rural Idaho. Ben and Amber Sessions thought that they had found the home of their dreams, but quickly realized that something was horribly wrong with it. Their home had been overrun with so many snakes that on one particular day they caught 43 of them. There were so many snakes that Amber confessed that "It felt like we were living in Satan's lair. . . . That's the only way to really explain it."

The family tried everything they could to stay in that house, deal with the snakes, but ultimately they were overrun and had to abandon their dream home. No matter how hard they tried to ignore all the snakes around them, it eventually became impossible.

Sometimes we have issues in our life that we have tried for a long time to ignore. Or perhaps we have tried to deal with the issues ourselves with little luck, as they seem to continue to fester. The reality is that there are issues in our lives that we need help with. Anxiety is often one of them. Sure, we can try our best to deal with the issues in the same way we have always done, while seeing few results. But maybe the time has come for us to reach out and get the help that we are longing for.

Stigmas

It doesn't take me to tell you that there are certain stigmas in many parts of our Christian culture about seeking professional help, especially when it comes to an issue such as anxiety. What makes this stigma all the more difficult is that each community has its own set of rules regarding not only what they think about the concept of anxiety in the first place, but also how one should proceed in dealing with it. Therefore, navigating the process can be difficult for many people.

Perhaps you are someone who is anxious but has chosen to ignore your ever-increasing anxiety because of fear or shame. You are not alone, and there are others who want to help you. Though she is speaking specifically about depression, I like the words of Mattie Gerber from her July 2009 article in *Relevant* magazine, "Can 'Real' Christians Be Depressed?":

> Depression should be treated and can be put into remission through a course of psychoanalysis, cognitive therapy and/or antidepressant medication, supplemented by healthy doses of prayer within a loving Christian community. It is nonsensical to tell a depressed person that if he only read his Bible more or had better quiet times, his depression would surely be lifted. That would be like telling a diabetic that faith alone will regulate her insulin levels. Faith alone gives eternal salvation, but in the meantime, God has given us resources by which to make our temporal existences more palatable. Depression is certainly healed by the grace of God, sometimes directly and miraculously, but more often through the tools of His servants, like pharmacists, therapists, pastors and friends.[2]

As a Christian community we have to approach an issue such as anxiety with a more holistic approach because what may work for one person may not work for another. Sometimes anxiety may be present in someone's life at such a low level that all they need is to read their Bible, recite a passage of Scripture, or say a prayer to feel that anxiety slowly fade away. Sometimes anxiety is present in someone's life to such a degree that spiritual practices, or attempts at healthier living and more exercise are not helping. Those people often reach out and seek the help of a therapist who can guide them through their anxiety. And sometimes someone's anxiety is so debilitating that nothing seems to work. They panic and live in a constant state of anxiousness, and something more radical like medication or inpatient treatment is needed. Anxiety is diverse just like the population of people that it affects. In any case, everyone faces anxiety at varying points in their lives, and the question is how to reach out when the time comes to seek the help of others.

As I have stated throughout this book, reimagining the role of anxiety in our lives is such an important concept that we must always be aware of how anxiety is manifesting itself in our lives and what God is saying to us in the midst of it.

Perhaps up to this point you are having a difficult time reimagining the role of anxiety in your life, and you have no idea how God could use it, or if He could, what He would even say.

That is okay.

Maybe, just maybe, you have come to the place where anxiety is the catalyst that is pushing you to take the next step and get the help you need. As a community of believers we need one another to walk through life, and God has placed men and women in your life who are gifted and who have been trained to come alongside of you and to help you on your journey with anxiety.

But I know that to come to this place where you realize that you can't do it on your own may be a very frightening thing. I understand that. That is a normal reaction.

But what would it look like to just let go of the burden you have been shouldering all alone for so long? What would it look like to have someone come alongside of you in this journey so that you can navigate it effectively?

You have made it this far. Let's take another step together and help you get the help that you need.

Finding a Therapist/Counselor

Resources for Finding Help

There are a lot of people who desire to go to a counselor, or at least try it out. Maybe you are one of them. But if you have never reached out to a counselor before, more than likely the process can be pretty scary. It takes a lot of courage to face our anxiety head-on and to reach out and seek the help that we are longing for. The good news is that you are not alone. Thousands of people call up counselors and counseling offices every day.

Possibly it would help if you knew a little more information about what to look for. Perhaps having some criteria to base your decision on would take some of the stress out of the process. There are many ways to go about this, but I want to share with you some suggestions that have helped me in my own process of looking for a therapist, and have helped many others in the process as well.

Reputation

This is a really great way to find a therapist. And by reputation, I mean those therapists' names that you have heard before, or have been recommended by others. Any time you are situated in a community (church, work, family) there are certain names, in certain professions or services, that one tends to hear over and over again. That's what I mean by reputation. There are therapists in different parts of the country who I tend to refer people to because of their reputation.

Personal Referral

Personal referrals are a really great resource for finding a good therapist, and a strong motivator for helping take that extra step needed to make that first phone call, schedule that first appointment, and walk into that first therapy session. This is the recommendation that comes from a personal friend or family member. More often than not, the person who makes this recommendation has been to see this person in therapy themselves, or is connected with others who have. Lots of great therapists build strong referral bases primarily on this source of recommendation.

Professional Referral

It is well known that pastors, teachers, doctors, psychiatrists, and other people who work in education, social and health care, and related fields can be great sources for referrals for people who are looking for a therapist. These professionals, and ones like them, have had a strong history of providing names of good therapists for people. I know many church attendees who wouldn't think of asking anyone but their pastor, or some person on their church staff about where to find a good therapist.

Social Media Crowdsourcing[3]

By *crowdsourcing*, I am referring to the practice of going online and asking people's opinions via resources like Twitter, Facebook, Yelp, Yahoo groups, "mommy" blogs, and other online tools that can provide good and practical insight to readers. In 2009 I received my first client via Twitter, and since then Twitter and Facebook have been a huge resource in helping people connect with me for therapy. Social media crowdsourcing is another way that those who I interact with online contact me to ask my opinion on a referral for them or someone else in another geographical location.

Online

Outside of the personal recommendation, I think the majority of people find a therapist online, whether it be through a website or social media. Obviously this is not a guarantee that who you find will be a good therapist, or someone that you connect with, but it's a good way to locate people in your area. I recommend going online and using a therapist locator tool (for example: therapistlocator.net, mytherapistmatch.com, or goodtherapy.org), browsing the lists of national or state professional licensing boards (for example: AAMFT.org), or ministry organizations that provide mental health care (for example: AMFMonline.com, AACC.net, AAPC.org). If a therapist has a website that is a great way to get a better sense of who the therapist is and what kind of therapy they provide.

Criteria for a Counselor/Therapist

Now that I have made a few suggestions about finding a good therapist let's talk about some things you should be looking for. This is going to differ based on a lot of factors, but I think most often, it will differ based on your history of how you have chosen therapists before, or how the community you are most active in goes about handling this process.

Though criteria may vary, here are some things that I think are important.

Education

Have they gone to school (undergraduate/graduate) to receive training for this profession? Or have they been through some sort of recognized and approved training program? If you are going to have the courage to step out and take the risk to find a therapist and commit to the process you want to know that they are qualified to deliver the services you are seeking.

Credentials

Besides education, what other credentials do they carry that enhance their work in this profession? Are they licensed through the national and state organizations? Have they attended training workshops that provided them with additional training tools, skill sets, or special certifications?

License

Are they licensed by the state they practice in? This could vary, as some great therapists don't carry a state license, but are instead certified by an organization (the AAPC and AACC are examples), and then they are usually monitored by some governing body such as a church or nonprofit organization. When looking online, look for a therapist's license number which is often displayed. If it is not, you may ask for their license number to verify their license. When a therapist is licensed through the state, some of the more common licenses you may see are LMFT, LSW, LPC, PhD, PsyD, usually with their license number following it.

Accountability

If a therapist is not licensed through the state, or is not certified through some governing board that provides oversight then be careful. There are plenty of horror stories of people who have gone to therapy with someone who was not practicing therapy under a proper set of ethical guidelines. But in cases like this there is often no recourse if there is no governing or licensing organization that supervises the practice of these therapists.

Experience

Does this person have experience in doing therapy, or experience in the specific areas that you are wanting to go see them for? Experience level obviously varies from therapist to therapist, and there are great therapists with all levels of experience. But do they meet your expectations?

Ethics

Does the therapist have a community (licensing board, pastoral care team, etc.) that they are accountable to for how they practice their therapy? Does the therapist seem to operate ethically in the manner that is appropriate for their profession?

Rapport

Do you connect? This is a key factor in how people determine if a therapist is right for them or not. But rapport does not mean that a client always likes what they hear from their therapist or that there aren't times of conflict and anxiety in the therapeutic relationship. A good therapist will be honest, even when the truth is hard to hear.

Do They Go to Therapy Themselves?

This is difficult to determine prior to finding a therapist, or even during the course of therapy. But I have found it to be a good rule of thumb to see a therapist who goes to therapy themselves (they may not currently be in therapy, but they attend on occasion to continue their own work, which makes them a better therapist). Therapists can still be good and not go to therapy themselves, but this is something that I have found helpful to myself and others.

Presence

Perhaps nothing is worse than a person finally taking the leap to go see a therapist and feeling like the therapist is tuned out, or not fully present with the client in the session. As a client you are paying for this person to be fully present with you in order that they can help you. I'm reminded of Ronald Rolheiser's words that "my vocation is, at each moment, to make the person in front of me the most important person in my life!"[4]

The Process

Sometimes people go to therapy just to talk. Sometimes people go to therapy to seek a solution. Whatever the reasons you go, it can be helpful if at some point during the process (usually in the first few sessions) the therapist can lay out some objectives, goals, or possible timelines for therapy. The process varies though, depending on a variety of factors from the therapist, to the theoretical model practiced, and to whether or not someone pays out of pocket or goes through insurance.

Spirituality

In the course of my life I have sought the help of both Christian and non-Christian therapists. And in the process they have both been helpful. I am reminded of the early church father Justin Martyr who believed that "all truth is God's truth." Whether a therapist is a Christian or not a Christian, there are certain truths about relationships, anxiety, and other aspects of human behavior that are just true. I think what is important is that you find a therapist who is willing to explore the spiritual life with you, regardless of their own views. All that being said, my own belief is that I want to work with someone who approaches my therapy taking into consideration my entire created being—spiritual, psychological, emotional, physical, relational, and more. Whether we agree on every theological issue is beside the point. But you must find someone that you are comfortable working with, but who will at the same time challenge you to think beyond what you are anxious about.

Anxiety, Christians, and Medication

When it comes to the issue of taking medication for anxiety there are some Christians who believe in it, and those who do not.

I believe in the use of medication.

I'm not trying to convince you otherwise. That will require circumstances and experiences beyond my control.

It's not the only tool that I may recommend for people, but it's one of the tools that may be helpful for people along with counseling.

I have worked long enough in the ministry and therapeutic setting to see the amazing and beneficial results that medications have had in the lives of the coworkers, students, and clients that I have journeyed through life with.

I believe God has given scientists, doctors, and researchers amazing minds to create some medications that can help.

As one friend says, "If someone is diabetic, they are going to take insulin, aren't they?"

Or I tell my friends, "If you have a heart condition, you are going to the cardiologist, right?"

So what's the stigma around mental health and medications in the Christian life?

I'm not completely sure. There is some disconnect it seems. Or rather than disconnect, there is some inconsistency in how we pick and choose what areas of our lives we seek help for with the use of medications, and in what areas we think we should be able to pick ourselves up by our own bootstraps and forgo medications.

If God has gifted a researcher who can create helpful drugs, or a psychiatrist who can prescribe medications, why not seek their help?

If God has gifted general practitioners and therapists to walk alongside of us in rough times, why not seek their help?

I've heard some people say to others who experience anxiety that they just need to read their Bibles more, or pray harder, or have better quiet times, or stop sinning. That has got to stop. Would you tell a cancer patient they should just pray harder, seek God more truthfully, and stop sinning? Some may, but I would tell them to go see an oncologist and get into some chemotherapy and/or radiation treatment.

Until we have struggled with anxiety ourselves, helped someone walk through that season, or been in a relationship or family where someone struggles with it, then the reality is often far removed from one's true understanding of just exactly how serious it can be. Instead, we play Monday morning, armchair quarterback, and give abstract principles, or methods of coping that don't seriously get at the heart of the issue.

What I have come to believe is that many of those Christians who think we should not take medications for mental health issues will truly never "get it," unless it strikes close to home.

Take Courage in the Face of Your Anxiety

So maybe you have come to this place of confronting your anxiety but you just aren't sure what to do or where to go. Take courage in knowing that you have done more in beginning to even look at the role of anxiety in your life than most people will ever do. Do not minimize the fact that you have made it this far.

Hopefully you are in a community of relationships that do not put up roadblocks, place labels, or produce stigmas around you getting the help that you need and that God has encouraged you to get.

We don't know why at varying times in our lives we experience anxiety, or why it is even present. But I do believe that God has a role in that anxiety, and that He is wanting you to boldy enter into the process of reimagining your anxiety in a healthy, life-giving way, rather than in a way that allows you to stuff it inside and debilitates you in the process.

As you move forward remember that anxiety in many ways is mysterious, but in that place we encounter a mysterious God who wants to transform you. Rob Bell in his book *Velvet Elvis* honestly shares about his own journey toward counseling:

In addition, there is always a mystery behind the mystery. There is a reason we do what we do, and often it is the result of something that is the result of something that is—you guessed it—the result of something. What happens is we try to fix things, but we stop at the first or second layer.

We're stressed and so we make adjustments in time management. But a better question is, why do I take on so much? But an ever better question is, why is it so hard for me to say no? Or even, why is that person's approval so important to me?

But that's not even the real issue.

> What I have learned is that the deeper you go, the more painful it gets.
> We have to be willing to drag everything up.
> I started going to counseling and discovered that there are things that happened to me when I was thirteen that have shaped me.
> Thirteen?[5]

There are things in your life that have shaped you as well. Seek the help you need to better understand how those things that have shaped you have created anxiety, and how you might best use that anxiety to birth new life in you.

acknowledgments

On July 13, 2010, four days after the birth of our second child, I received an email that I at first thought was a joke. It was from Randall Payleitner, who stated that he was the acquisitions editor for spiritual formation for Moody Publishers in Chicago. He had apparently stumbled across my blog, was intrigued, and was curious if I would pursue some ideas with him for possible publication. So I want to start by thanking Randall for reaching out to me and giving me the chance. He has been supportive throughout the writing process. Thanks for your encouragement. This book has seen the light of day because of your effort.

I would also like to thank the entire Moody staff I have had the privilege to work with. I could not have asked for a better team. Thank you, Chris Reese, for taking my words and bringing them to life on the page. Your direction in editing the manuscript has been invaluable. I also want to thank the marketing team of Duane Sherman, Ashley High, Natalie

Myers, and Andrew Allen. A week did not pass during the entire writing process where one of you wasn't following up on my progress and helping me take the steps I needed to take for this book to successfully launch off the shelves and into people's hands. I want to thank Brittany Biggs for taking care of all the necessary paperwork and making sure that I was doing the small things that would have a huge impact on helping this book get published. Finally, I want to thank the video work of Josue Reyes. He took what meager talent I had in front of the video camera and helped bring my story to life. Again, thank you to Moody and the entire team who was behind the process of *The Anxious Christian* from beginning to end. You made writing (both the good and bad days) a joy. I am humbled by your work and care with my writing and I have forever learned the lesson that writers who publish only do so because there is an amazing team of people walking alongside of them.

There are so many people to thank that I cannot possibly mention each and every one of you. That would take more pages than this entire book. I hope to be able to thank you in person one day over a cup of coffee.

I want to thank the Fuller Theological Seminary community. My time as both an MDiv student ('03) and MSMFT student ('07) were life transforming to me as a person. Thanks for caring for me and allowing me to explore my faith in a challenging and safe environment.

I want to thank Bel Air Presbyterian Church in Los Angeles. My seven years there as the college pastor and intern ('01–'08) shaped me in profound ways. I owe special thanks not only to the staff, but to all of the amazing college students and leadership teams who so gracefully allowed me to serve alongside of them . . . stutters and all.

I want to thank everyone involved at The Hideaway Experience in Amarillo, Texas. Being on staff as one of the marriage therapists there has been more transformative for my own life and marriage than just about anything I can think of.

I am thankful to be blessed with a lot of great friends who have continually encouraged me on this journey. I especially want to thank all of you who have daily been walking alongside of me the last few years and whose presence has been solace for my own anxiety.

A writer needs other writer friends to lament to. So I'm thankful too for all my author friends who so patiently gave me constructive criticism and encouragement in just the right balance. You helped me plod forward when I thought my manuscript was better left in the trash.

Thank you, Explosions in the Sky, for pretty much motivating me through the writing and editing of an entire book. Your music was inspirational.

I want to thank my family. You have all believed in me from beginning to end. I talk a lot in the book about how we are shaped in life by our family of origin, so I am thankful every day that I was raised in a loving home by loving parents. And if that were not enough, through my marriage, God blessed me as well with a wonderful extended family. Thank you for all your support, prayers, and encouragement.

To my wife and kids, I owe you everything. For without

you, there would be no book. Writing and editing day in and day out is a very self-absorbed process. So it is not lost on me that without the love, patience, and grace of my amazing wife, Heather, there would be no *The Anxious Christian* to read. Heather, though you know I am the most talkative and wordy person around, there are still not enough words I could say or write that would adequately convey just how much you mean to me. You have taught me what it means to live in grace and to love unconditionally. Thank you for all your encouragement in this writing process. Your thoughtful attention to my ideas and writing was crucial in helping bring this book to life. This book is as much yours as it is mine. I want to thank my daughter Hayden and my son Hudson who are daily reminders to live courageously, face our fears, and take risks. I love you all so much.

Thank You to my Lord and Savior Jesus Christ who has continually walked beside me through the darkest of nights and the brightest of days. You have taught me to face my anxieties, and when I do You have been there to turn them into something beautiful in my life.

notes

Dedication

1. Miguel de Unamuno, *Tragic Sense of Life*, trans. J. E. Crawford Fitch (New York: Cosimo, 2005), 193.

Introduction: The Day I Became a Stutterer

1. M. Scott Peck, *The Road Less Traveled: A New Psychology of Love, Traditional Values and Spiritual Growth* (New York: Simon and Schuster, 1978), 15.

2. Emmy Van Duerzen and Raymond Kenward, *The Dictionary of Existential Psychotherapy and Counseling* (Thousand Oaks: Sage Publications, 2005), 6.

3. Quoted in Rollo May, *The Meaning of Anxiety* (New York: Norton, 1977), 37.

4. *The King's Speech*, directed by Tom Hooper (The Weinstein Company and UK Film Council, 2010).

Chapter 1: Embracing Anxiety

1. C. S. Lewis, *The Lion, the Witch, and the Wardrobe* (New York: MacMillan, 1974), 75.

2. Ibid., 75–76.

3. Rollo May, *The Meaning of Anxiety* (New York: Norton, 1977), xv.

4. I am indebted to D. Michael Smith, my Marriage and Family Therapy supervisor, for the formulation and application of these four important questions.

5. Irvin D. Yalom, *Existential Psychotherapy* (New York: Harper Collins, 1980), 8.

6. Leslie S. Greenberg, *Emotion-Focused Therapy: Coaching Clients to Work Through Their Feelings* (Washington D.C.: American Psychological Association, 2002), 143.

7. Edmund J. Bourne, *The Anxiety and Phobia Workbook* (Oakland: New Harbinger Publications, 2010), 175–77.

8. Ibid., 175. "Usually this is the strongest subpersonality in people who are prone to anxiety. The Worrier creates anxiety by imagining the worst-case scenarios. It scares you with fantasies of disaster or catastrophe when you imagine confronting something you fear."

9. Ibid., 176. "The Critic is the part of you which is constantly judging and evaluating your behavior. It tends to point out your flaws and limitations whenever possible. It jumps on any mistake you make to remind you that you are a failure."

10. Ibid., 176. "The Victim is that part of you which feels helpless or hopeless. It generates anxiety by telling you that you're not making any progress, that your condition is incurable, or that the road is too long and steep for you to have a real chance at recovering. The Victim also plays a major role in creating depression. The Victim believes that there is something inherently wrong with you: you are in some ways deprived, defective, or unworthy."

11. Ibid., 176–77. "The Perfectionist is a close cousin of the Critic, but its concern is less to put you down than to push and goad you to do better. It generates anxiety by constantly telling you that your efforts aren't good enough, that you should be working harder, that you should always have everything under control, should always be competent, should always be pleasing, should always be _____. The Perfectionist is the hard-driving part of you that wants to be best and is intolerant of mistakes or setbacks. It has a tendency to try to convince you that your self-worth is dependent on externals such as vocational achievement, money and status, acceptance by others, being loved, or your consistent ability to be pleasing and nice to others regardless of what they do."

Notes

Chapter 2: Welcoming Uncertainty

1. T. S. Eliot, *Four Quartets* (San Diego: Harcourt, 1971), 29.

2. William Bridges, *Transitions: Making Sense of Life's Changes* (Cambridge: De Capo, 2004), xii.

3. Eugene Peterson, *Eat This Book: A Conversation in the Art of Spiritual Reading* (Grand Rapids: Eerdmans, 2006), 9.

4. See Walter Brueggemann, *The Message of the Psalms* (Minneapolis: Augsburg Fortress, 1984).

5. Ibid., 19. "Human life consists in satisfied seasons of well-being that evoke gratitude for the constancy of blessing." (For example, Psalm 1, 8, etc.)

6. Ibid. "Human life consists in anguished seasons of hurt, alienation, suffering, and death. These evoke rage, resentment, self-pity, and hatred." (For example, Psalm 13, 86, etc.)

7. Ibid. "Human life consists in turns of surprise when we are overwhelmed with the new gifts of God, when joy breaks through despair." (For example, Psalm 30, 40, etc.)

8. Ibid., 22.

9. Eugene Peterson, *The Pastor* (New York: Harper Collins, 2011), 4. Peterson is quoting from the poem "Overland to the Islands" by Denise Levertov.

10. R. A. Guelich and J. O. Hagberg, *The Critical Journey: Stages in the Life of Faith* (Salem, WI: Sheffield, 1995), xxii.

11. M. Scott Peck, *The Road Less Traveled: A New Psychology of Love, Traditional Values and Spiritual Growth* (New York: Simon and Schuster, 1978).

12. I learned this concept from my father, Timothy Smith, at the Bel Air Presbyterian Church college group (The Quest) retreat he was speaking at in 2002. You can learn more about the work of Timothy Smith by visiting Water from Rock (www.waterfromrock.org).

Chapter 3: Stuck in a Rut

1. Ian Cron, *Jesus, My Father, The CIA, and Me: A Memoir of Sorts* (Nashville: Thomas Nelson, 2011), 94.

2. Brent J. Atkinson, "Supplementing Couples Therapy with Methods for Reconditioning Emotional Habits," *Family Therapy Magazine* May/June (2011): 29. Atkinson writes, "Brain studies suggest that across their lifetimes, people develop internal mechanisms for coping with things that are upsetting to them. The brain organizes these coping mechanisms into coherent, self-protective neural response programs that are highly automated (Panksepp, 1998). Once a neural response program forms, each time it is triggered, a predictable pattern of thoughts, urges and actions unfold. Neural response programs can dramatically bias people's perceptions and interpretations without them realizing it, and generate powerful inclinations to attack, defend, or retreat."

3. From Robert Frost's poem "The Road Not Taken."

4. Terry D. Hargrave and Franz Pfitzer, *Restoration Therapy: Understanding and Guiding Healing in Marriage and Family Therapy* (New York: Routledge, 2011), 3.

5. Terry Hargrave, *The Essential Humility of Marriage: Honoring the Third Identity in Couple Therapy* (Phoenix: Zeig, Tucker and Theisen, 2000), 72–74.

6. See Monica McGoldrick, Randy Gerson, and Sueli Petry, *Genograms: Assessment and Intervention* (New York: Norton, 2008).

7. Chaim Potok, *My Name is Asher Lev* (New York: Ballantine, 1972), 289.

8. Drew Sams, "The Re-Membered Church: Establishing and Enacting a Narrative Ecclesiology in a New Media World" (forthcoming doctoral dissertation, George Fox Evangelical Seminary, 2012).

9. Howard Stone, *Depression and Hope: New Insights for Pastoral Counseling* (Minneapolis: Augsburg Fortress, 1998), 47–48.

10. Hargrave and Pfitzer, 154.

11. Cron, 101.

12. See Hargrave and Pfitzer's *Restoration Therapy* (cited above) for a helpful list of common feelings and coping behaviors, especially pages 44 and 50.

Notes

Chapter 4: Anxiety Reimagined

1. Quoted in Arne Gron, *The Concept of Anxiety in Søren Kierkegaard* (Macon, GA: Mercer University Press, 2008), 19.

2. N. T. Wright, *Surprised by Hope: Rethinking Heaven, the Resurrection, and the Mission of the Church* (San Francisco: HarperOne, 2008), 40.

3. Eugene Peterson, *Christ Plays in Ten Thousand Places: A Conversation in Spiritual Theology* (Grand Rapids: Eerdmans, 2008), 230.

4. Dietrich Bonhoeffer, *Meditations on the Cross* (Louisville: Westminster John Knox, 1998), 79.

5. Irvin Yalom, *Existential Psychotherapy* (New York: Basic Books, 1980), 163.

6. *Gladiator*, directed by Ridley Scott (Dreamworks SKG, 2000).

7. Wilber F. Gingrich, *Shorter Lexicon of the Greek New Testament* (Chicago: University of Chicago Press, 1965), 134.

8. Rollo May, *The Meaning of Anxiety* (New York: Norton, 1977), 43.

9. Ibid.

10. Søren Kierkegaard, *Fear and Trembling* (Princeton: Princeton University Press, 1983), 30.

Chapter 5: Wrestling with God

1. Fyodor Dostoevsky, *Crime and Punishment*, trans. Constance Ganett (New York: P.F. Collier & Son, 1917), 2.

2. The Hideaway Marriage Experience (www.intensives.com) is a retreat center that facilitates marriage intensives for couples and trains ministry leaders to help transform marriages in their church through the use of the 5 Days to a New Marriage curriculum (www.5daystoanewmarriage.com).

3. Terry Hargrave and Shawn Stoever, *5 Days to a New Marriage* (Amarillo, TX: The Hideaway Foundation, 2011), 13ff.

4. The therapeutic model in *5 Days to a New Marriage* was developed at The Hideaway Marriage Experience.

5. Pain Cycle: negative cycle of interaction where a pattern is formed between feelings/emotions and the coping behaviors that result from it.

6. Peace Cycle: positive cycle of interaction where a pattern is formed between our truth and new actions/behaviors.

7. Terry D. Hargrave and Franz Pfitzer, *Restoration Therapy: Understanding and Guiding Healing in Marriage and Family Therapy* (New York: Routledge, 2011), 153.

8. Karl Barth, "The Knowledge of God and the Service of God According to the Teaching of the Reformtion, 1937–1938," Gifford Lectures, www.giffordlectures.org.

9. Phyllis Trible, *Texts of Terror: Literary-Feminist Readings of Biblical Narratives* (Minneapolis: Fortress, 1984), 4–5.

10. Henry Nouwen, *In the Name of Jesus: Reflections on Christian Leadership* (New York: Crossroad, 1989), 15ff.

11. Hargrave and Pfitzer, 122.

12. Ibid., 123.

Chapter 6: Getting Intentional

1. Steven Pressfield, *Do the Work* (The Domino Project, 2011), Kindle edition.

2. Jack Kent, *There's No Such Thing as a Dragon* (New York: Dragonfly Books, 2009), 1, 4, 24.

3. Pressfield, Kindle edition.

4. The Hideaway Experience, http://www.intensives.com.

5. Thanks to Dr. Terry Hargrave for introducing this story at the Hideaway Experience and the insights and implications it has for change in a marriage.

6. David Ford, *The Shape of Living: Spiritual Directions for Everyday Life* (Grand Rapids: Baker, 2004), 33.

7. Thomas Moore, *A Life at Work: The Joy of Discovering What You Were Born to Do* (New York: Three Rivers Press, 2009), 29–30.

8. *Chariots of Fire*, directed by Hugh Hudson (Allied Stars Ltd., 1981).

9. Eugene Peterson, *Eat This Book: A Conversation in the Art of Spiritual Reading* (Grand Rapids: Eerdmans, 2009), 70–71.

10. Quoted in J. P. Moreland, *Love God with All Your Mind* (Colorado Springs: NavPress, 1997), 28.

11. Ann Voskamp, *One Thousand Gifts: A Dare to Live Fully Right Where You Are* (Grand Rapids: Zondervan, 2011).

12. Dietrich Bonhoeffer, *Meditating on the Word* (Boston: Cowley, 2000), 51.

13. This is an exercise my dad taught me.

Chapter 7: Creating Boundaries and Space

1. Rainer Maria Rilke, *Letters to a Young Poet* (Boston: Harvard University Press, 2011), 71.

2. Henry Cloud and John Townsend, *Boundaries: When to Say Yes, How to Say No to Take Control of Your Life* (Grand Rapids: Zondervan, 1992), 29–30.

3. Melody Beatie, *Beyond Codependency: And Getting Better All the Time* (Center City, MN: Hazelden, 1989), 173.

4. Marva Dawn, *Keeping the Sabbath Wholly: Ceasing, Resting, Embracing, Feasting* (Grand Rapids: Eerdmans, 1989), 23.

5. Henry Nouwen, *Reaching Out: The Three Movements of the Spiritual Life* (New York: Image Books, 1986), 52–53.

6. Ibid., 51–52.

7. Irvin Yalom, *The Theory and Practice of Group Psychotherapy* (New York: Basic Books, 2000), 94.

8. Barry Schwartz, *The Paradox of Choice: Why More Is Less* (San Francisco: Harper Perennial, 2005), 2–3.

9. Parker J. Palmer. *Let Your Life Speak: Listening for the Voice of Vocation* (Hoboken, NJ: Jossey-Bass, 1999), 15–16.

Chapter 8: Relational Refinement

1. Dietrich Bonhoeffer, *Creation and Fall: A Theological Exposition of Genesis 1–3* (Minneapolis: Augsburg Fortress, 1997), 63.

2. Miroslav Volf, *After Our Likeness: The Church as the Image of the Trinity* (Grand Rapids: Eerdmans, 1998), 209.

3. My parents gave me the middle name Travis after Lieutenant Colonel William Barret Travis who died at the battle of the Alamo. Upon realizing that their situation looked bleak, on March 4, 1836, Travis told the other soldiers, "We must die. Our business is not to make a fruitless effort to save our lives, but to choose the manner of our death." Travis then took his sword, drawing a line in the sand at the Alamo, asking those who wanted to stay and fight to stay, and those who didn't to leave.

4. David Schnarch, *Passionate Marriage: Keeping Love and Intimacy Alive in Committed Relationships* (New York: Norton, 2009).

5. Terry Hargrave, *The Essential Humility of Marriage: Honoring the Third Identity in Couple Therapy* (Phoenix: Zeig, Tucker and Theisen, 2000), 150.

6. Parker Palmer, *A Hidden Wholeness: The Journey Toward an Undivided Life* (Hoboken, NJ: Jossey-Bass, 2009), 55.

7. Dietrich Bonhoeffer, *Sanctorum Communio: A Theological Study of the Sociology of the Church* (Minneapolis: Augsburg Fortress, 1998), 52.

8. Schnarch, 55.

9. Elaine Cook, "The Sexual Crucible and Imago Relationship Therapy: Two Approaches to Marital Counseling," http://aphroweb.net.

10. Terry Hargrave, *The Essential Humility of Marriage: Honoring the Third Identity in Couple Therapy* (Phoenix: Zeig, Tucker and Theisen, 2000).

11. Rainer Maria Rilke, *Letters to a Young Poet* (Boston: Harvard University Press, 2011), 63.

12. Eugene Peterson in *Christ Plays in Ten Thousand Places: A Conversation in Spiritual Theology* (Grand Rapids: Eerdmans, 2008), 231.

Appendix: Reaching for Help

1. Rhett Smith, "Depression and Burnout: Anne Jackson Interview, Part 1," www.rhettsmith.com, http://rhettsmith.com/2009/07/depression-and-burnout-anne-jackson-interview-part-1/.

2. *Relevant*, "Can 'Real' Christians Be Depressed?" http://www.relevant magazine.com/life/whole-life/features/1976-can-qrealq-christians-be-depressed.

3. Crowdsourcing "is the act of outsourcing tasks, traditionally performed by an employee or contractor, to an undefined, large group of people or community (a 'crowd'), through an open call." http://en.wikipedia.org/wiki/Crowdsourcing.

4. Ronald Rolheiser, *The Restless Heart: Finding Our Spiritual Home in Times of Loneliness* (New York: Doubleday, 2004), 23.

5. Rob Bell, *Velvet Elvis: Repainting the Christian Faith* (Grand Rapids: Zondervan, 2005), 111–12.

How to Ruin Your Life by 30

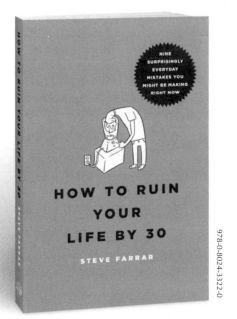

Everyone has an internal alarm clock that goes off when they're about to make a bad decision. Some men and women spend their twenties hitting the snooze button. Steve Farrar gives them the wake-up call that they can't escape, to help them avoid the life-shattering consequences of foolish choices. Upon speaking at Biola University, Steve Farrar made an instant connection with the students, generating tremendous response. This book springs out of their burning questions and struggles. It helps young men and women prevent mistakes before they make them, but it also can help readers recover from poor choices before it's too late.

MOODY
Publishers™

From the Word to Life

MoodyPublishers.com

The Road Trip that Changed the World

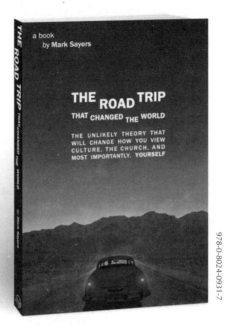

Sixty years ago a goatee beard would have gotten you beat up in a lot of places. Chin fuzz was the symbol of the Beats or Beatniks, a mid-century, marginal group who pioneered a new kind of lifestyle that was hedonistic, experiential, and individualistic. Their contradictory approach to spirituality combined a search for God with a search for "kicks." In 1947, these Beatnik heroes set out on a road trip across America rewriting the "life-script" of all future generations. They modeled a new approach to faith: desiring Christ, while still pursuing a laundry list of vices. Yet this dream would turn into a nightmare, and the open road would lead back to an ancient, half-forgotten path. It was a path that began with a single step of faith as a pilgrim named Abraham stepped away from a cynical culture. A path of devotion that led to a cross on Golgotha.

MOODY Publishers™

*From the Word **to** Life*

MoodyPublishers.com

Honest to God

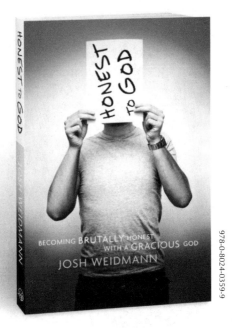

Is hypocrisy eroding your trust in relationships, the church, or even yourself? We long to know there is a God—and, yes, a community—who is big enough to accept us for who we are and loving enough not to leave us that way. Imagine how our relationships and witness would change if Christians everywhere began to live in a more authentic manner. Throughout the Bible, we find heroes of the faith who lived with daring, messy honesty before God and others. *Honest to God* is a practical and riveting study of biblical honesty. Follow next-generation author, Josh Weidmann, as he takes the reader on a journey toward true Christian authenticity. Both biblical and contemporary examples will give you practical principles and tools for self-examination that will lead to the freedom and transformation that come only through honesty with God.

MOODY
Publishers™

From the Word to Life

MoodyPublishers.com